THE END IS COME

Book 1

AN ONLY EVIL, BEHOLD, IT IS COME

Book 2

WHO CHANGED GOD'S NAME?

apocalypsehouse.com

THE END IS COME

AN ONLY EVIL, BEHOLD, IT IS COME

WHO CHANGED GOD'S NAME?

APPROACHING DOOM

AND THE GREAT DECEPTION

by

Norbert H. Kox

"LOVE"

אהב

AHB

Apocalypse House Books

New Franken, WI

THE END IS COME

AN ONLY EVIL, BEHOLD, IT IS COME!
WHO CHANGED GOD'S NAME?

ISBN: 978-0-6151-6141-9

Library of Congress Control Number: 2007936939

Please visit our website: www.apocalypsehouse.com

For information regarding author interviews, please contact:
nhkox@yahoo.com

Cover design and all artwork by Norbert H. Kox

Cover image: Death of Babylon (detail, digitally altered color)

Printed in the United States of America

Apocalypse House

New Franken, WI

DEDICATION

This book is dedicated to the glory and honor of Yesu, and to my very close friend and lifelong colleague Keith W. Kraus (Bud). He was the proofreader of *Six Nights till Morning: The Real Star Wars*, which included the first printing of "Who Changed God's Name."

Bud is a true brother. Together, he and I came into the truths of the Sabbath and the Name. We were so struck by the importance that on March 6, 1982, in 20-degree weather, we shoveled two feet of snow off a creek in Northern Wisconsin and chopped a hole through 12 inches of solid ice, to re-baptize each other by immersion in the name of Yesu Christ. It was the greatest day in our lives.

In the more than twenty-five years to follow, we have each faced great obstacles, challenges and tribulations. New struggles arise each day. May we persevere till the end.

God bless all my brothers and sisters, in Bimini and around the world, along with everyone who puts his hands on this book and sets his heart to contemplate these writings.

You are already on the Path, and the "secret" name of the Creator is already upon your lips.

ACKNOWLEDGEMENTS

My first thanks go to God, who commissioned this work and guided my research. With warm thanks and humble gratitude, I commend all my diligent proofreaders. Special thanks to Jeremy J. Kox for all of his encouragement and consultation. Thanks to K.W. Kraus and George E. Meyer for their continual involvement in this great endeavor. Thanks to Pastor Edmond Ellis (Community Church of God, Bimini, Bahamas) for his diligent proofreading, comments and suggestions. Thanks also to my beloved artist friend, Anna Sea, of Brooklyn, New York, for her valuable input. Very special thanks to Nancy Kolosso, who did the original typing of *Six Nights Till Morning: The Real Star*

Wars, the 900-page manuscript in which "Who Changed God's Name" appeared for the first time (c. 1983).

OTHER TITLES TO WATCH FOR
by Norbert H. Kox

The Yod of God: Returning His Name, Recovering His Remnant

Masquerade: Antichrist is Here

The White Lie

The Woman's Tail: The Real Star Wars

Sapphire Sphere: Portal to Eternity

Onyx Stones: Key of the Portal

Bimini: The Top of God's Mountain

Sound the Shofar

Check for availability at Apocalypse House
http://nkox.homestead.com/BooksByNHK.html
http://apocalypsehouse.com

"LOVE"

אהב

AHB

Apocalypse House Books

Satan disguises as an Angel of Light (2 Corinthians 11:14).

The Wrong Comforter

acrylic and oil

by Norbert H. Kox

FOREWORD

The Adversary constantly works to counterfeit the true message of God.

Satan, as Lucifer, said, "I shall be like the Most High, I shall sit also upon the *Mount of the Congregation.*" That is *Har Moad* in Hebrew, and *Har Megeddo* or *Armageddon* in Greek. In this prophecy of Isaiah 14:12-14, and in many other Scripture verses, the Adversary makes it clear that he will infiltrate the congregation and be worshiped as God and Saviour. His struggle to do so is literally the battle of Armageddon.

The Mystery of Iniquity, better translated "the Secret of Lawlessness," spoken of in 2Thessalonians 2:3-12, is Satan imitating and appearing as Christ. We see in 2Corinthians 11:14-15, that this secret applies to both Satan and his duped followers, masquerading as servants of Christ and ministers of righteousness. Scripture says the appearance of Antichrist is according to the "energy" of Satan (2Thessalonians 2:9, from the Greek).

The Luciferian initiation is when someone receives the energy (*energeia*) of the satans, believing it is the light of God. This person will be in the service of the Antichrist ("instead-of-Christ") believing he is doing a service to God (cf. John 16:2-3).

We must be extremely cautious, alert and aware, for the secret of lawlessness, the mystery of iniquity, is undoubtedly at work in our time.

(*The Yod of God: Returning His Name, Recovering His Remnant*, Kox).

APPROACHING OUR DOOM

An horrendous destruction is about to consume the entire New York City area, which will have horrifying repercussions on the United States and the rest of the world. The devastation we are talking about will make 911 and Hurricane Katrina look like nothing. Prophecies of this great doom are recorded in the Bible, and their imminence is confirmed by the current warnings of seismologists and meteorologists.

This may be the heralding of God's admonition to come out of Mystery Babylon or be destroyed.

The following insights were 120 years ahead of time. They were not for 1890, but they are relevant to the precise scenario we are being faced with today:

> ...Tyre and Babylon and Nineveh were in full pomp and splendor when these prophecies, these old prophecies, said they would be destroyed. Those cities had architecture that make the houses on Madison Square and Fifth Avenue perfectly insignificant. Yet these old prophets walked right through those magnificent streets and said: "This has all got to come down; that is all going to be leveled."
>
> Suppose a man should stand up in these cities today and say: "**The East River will overflow and Brooklyn will be destroyed, and the Hudson River will overflow and New York will be destroyed; and then there will be a great earthquake and the two rivers will forsake their beds**, and there will be harvests of wheat and corn where these cities now stand, and Fulton Street and Broadway will be pasture for cattle." Such a man would be sent to Bloomingdale Insane Asylum. Yet the old prophets did that very thing. ...

(p. 61, *Trumpet Peals: A Collection of Timely and Eloquent Extracts from the Sermons of the Rev. T. De Witt Talmage, D.D.*, Broomfield & Company, New York, 1890).

What this man saw 120 years ago, is exactly what the seismologists and meteorologists see and predict today. It is also what was prophesied in the Bible thousands of years ago, for those who would decipher it in the last days.

THE AUTHOR

Norbert H. Kox has researched the Bible in its original languages for more than 30 years, and presents his startling findings in the form of artworks and writings. As a steward of Yesu Christ and a Visionary Artist, he paints Apocalyptic Visual Parables, with an undaunted zeal to expose religious counterfeits in the often painful light of raw truth.

Some people comment that my artwork is very disturbing, and filled with negative imagery. This is a good observation. My works are Apocalyptic Visual Parables and are mostly warnings. As such they are meant to shock and disturb. You can't tell someone there is a fire without shouting "Fire!" The initial impact can be horrifying, but the negative elements become positive when properly interpreted.

You would not see a flower or a butterfly on a poison bottle. The skull and cross bones appear with the word poison. This imagery and text seem negative, but when interpreted to mean, "do not drink this," the message and image become positive: it will save your life.

In the spiritual sense, my iconography operates in the same way.

My message focuses on exposing mistranslations, misconceptions, and lies, which have been fostered in great part by the religious, and specifically by Modern Christianity.

Whether in writing or artwork the message is often upsetting, simply because it forces us to examine things and to see and recognize the truth. Truth can be intense even frightening. And once that gate has been opened there is no turning away.

Mine is a ministry of salvation through warnings and admonishments, which expose deceptions and reveal truths. It is not my mission to judge individuals, or to tell people how to live. You are the one who has to decide what to believe or what to do. We have each been endowed with a personal conscience (with possible exception of people with certain mental conditions). If you are doing wrong, you probably already know it. No one has to tell you.

We must exercise free will to make our choices, good or bad. Our choices should be educated, not blind. If you want to do what is right, you must seek the truth and then make your own educated assessments and choices.

This dissertation is not intended to frighten, condemn or excuse anyone, but to reveal certain facts you have a right to know.

SHEMAH

"Shemah," means *hear, listen, understand, obey, announce, proclaim.* It is the Biblical confession proclaiming the Name and the Oneness of God, beginning in Deuteronomy 6:4.

The *Sh'mah* is the first and greatest Word:

"Hear O' Israel, Yahweh is our God. Yahweh is One."

"My people, surely you will rebirth."

The name/word Israel can be translated several ways:

He shall wrestle God

He will be God's ruler

He will be God's leader

He will be God's umbilical cord

He will sing of God

He shall see God

PRONUNCIATION

Most Jews, because of tradition will not pronounce the name of Yahweh or even the words Lord and God. In printed matter they simply write L-rd and G-d, indicating that it should not be pronounced. If you are Jewish, please do not take offense at the use of the Name Yahweh in this writing. As you read the section on Who Changed God's Name, you will soon understand the importance of pronouncing his name.

* CONTENTS *

THE END IS COME

BOOK 1

AN ONLY EVIL, BEHOLD, IT IS COME

THE CIPHER

DOOMSDAY NEW YORK

BOOK 2

WHO CHANGED GOD'S NAME?

UNFORGETTING THE FORGOTTEN

EPILOGUE

CONCLUSION AND CONVICTION

LAST WORD

YAHWEH YESU IN SCRIPTURE

NAKED TRUTH

YESU'S WAY AND ATTITUDE

"THE END IS COME"

The Source: Arc of the Ark, acrylic on canvas, NHK

THE END IS COME

BOOK 1

AN ONLY EVIL, BEHOLD, IT IS COME

THE CIPHER

RECORDED IN ADVANCE

The Bible Code Has recorded virtually every major incident and important historical event since the beginning of time; all written and recorded before they happened. **The September 11, terrorist attack on New York is accurately recorded in great detail. Another devastating tragedy is recorded for New York also. If it is accurate, like the other entries, it may prove to be the worst human suffrage since the great flood.** It could conceivably be a destruction from which the land will never recover. The damage may be irreparable. The Bible codes are warning us.

WHAT ARE THE BIBLE CODES?

The Bible Code is a scientific analysis of the Hebrew text of the Bible. When each letter is placed in a grid, the matrix becomes a cross-word puzzle, a word-search, with words and phrases interlocking in all directions, right, left, up, down, and diagonally.

The scientific principle which is incorporated into the Bible Code is what cryptographers refer to as equidistant letter sequence (ELS). It simply means that each letter in a code is an equal distance from its preceding letter. So if a code is on a five letter skip, every fifth letter is part of the code which spells out a word, or phrase, or sentence.

The Bible Code phenomenon has been known of for many centuries. Both ancient and modern scholars have worked with it meticulously counting out hundreds of letters by hand, to find the hidden messages that are encoded within the Hebrew text.

It is only in modern times, since the 1980s, that researchers have begun searching the code by means of computer, and only since the publishing of Michael Drosnin's book, *The Bible Code* (1997) that many of us have heard of its existence. Still today, the majority of people have never heard of it.

With an ELS, there may be a three-letter-skip, where every third letter is part of the code. If the skip is 100 letters, every hundredth letter is counted. In a 100-skip code each line has 100 letters in it. The matrix is found at the location of the key-word. The grid can then be searched for the presence of other words and phrases like a word search puzzle. Some Rabbis, scholars and scientists investigating the codes believe that the Bible (Torah/Tanach) is encoded with every event past, present and future. Thus it would also encode every person's name along with his or her history (the Book of Life). The assassination of Yitzhak Rabin was discovered in the Code, long before it happened, but it could not be prevented.

...Many books have been written about the Bible Code, and more are hitting the shelves each day. With all of these books the phenomenon should be well understood. But instead, it is becoming more of a blur, for the average person.

There are many misconceptions concerning the Bible Code, and some of the proponents of the code are just as damaging to its validity as the antagonists are.

(*The Yod of God: Returning His Name, Recovering His Remnant*, Kox).

"My face will I turn also from them, and they shall pollute *my secret place* [צפוני = my code]: and shall enter into it, robbers, and defile it." (Ezekiel 7:22). In plain English, this verse says, "I will also turn my face from them, and they shall pollute my secret place (*my code*) and robbers shall enter into it and defile it." This verse can be read two other ways. 1) "My face will I turn also from them, and they shall break my code, and *with lattice* [בארבה], violent men break it." 2) "My face will I turn also from them, and they shall break my code and *explain with it* [באר בה], violent men break it." (Ezekiel 7:22).

Those who are misusing the Code are the robbers, defiling it. They have broken, or opened, the codes "with lattice." This is exactly how the codes work. The Bible Code grid or matrix is a latticework of letters, interwoven with hidden messages.

They "break my code and explain with it." Who? "Violent men."

They use the Code to explain, but are mostly erroneous, because God has turned his face from them.

Scripture says, "the kingdom of heaven **suffereth violence**, and the **violent** take it by force." (Matthew 11:12). Does this refer to robbers trying to violently force their way into the kingdom? If the violent are the robbers, they are defiling the Code.

THE BIBLE IS THE CODE

The word Bible simply means Book. Our English word Bible comes from the Latin *biblia* and the Greek and Phoenician *byblos*, meaning "book." The Hebrew word for book or scroll ספר (SPhR) *sefar*, also means *to count* or *number*, and *to tell*, which is what the Code does. These same three Hebrew letters can be pronounced "cipher." In English a cipher is a secret code written in letters or characters that must be deciphered into intelligible terms by use of a key. Ancient rabbis found codes in the Scriptures. Their key was in equidistant letter sequences. Current researchers use the computer to unlock ELS codes.

The use of computer programs help researchers to discover the number skip-sequences, or ELS, at which God has encoded and "sealed the cipher" of his messages for his people to unravel and decode in the last days, "the time of the end ...when knowledge will be multiplied" (Daniel 12:4).

(*The Yod of God: Returning His Name, Recovering His Remnant*, Kox).

TREE OF LIFE PLAN

In Genesis 2:9, the nine Hebrew letters (בתוכהגנוע) located between the *tree of life* and the *tree of knowledge of good and evil*, "**in the midst/middle of the garden**," when **read in reverse** (עונגהכותב) translate into English as **"Delight of the Scribe."**

In unpointed script, the same two letters that spell

"tree" (עץ) also spell "plan." The tree of life and the tree of knowledge of good and evil may be **one** same tree in the middle of the garden. *The tree* is symbolic of *the Plan* of God, and as such it represents the Word of God, the Living Word, *the delight (enjoyment) of the scribe.*

The tree/plan/word of God encodes his secrets and reveals them to his scribes. (*ibid.*).

SYMMETRICAL CODES

When I first began working with Bible Codes, in 1997, I did everything by hand, counting out the Hebrew letters like the scribes of old and recording them on graph paper, then deciphering the grids like word puzzles. Everywhere I looked it said, "My symmetry." This told me immediately that God placed a great significance on symmetry in the codes. He has always used symmetry in the Scriptures in many overt references, so it should be no surprise that he would use symmetry in the hidden codes as well.

There are an endless number of significant codes that are asymmetrical, but the symmetrical codes are especially meaningful, adding another level of complexity to the already complex system of cryptological ciphers. (*ibid.*).

The codes virtually reveal encrypted details of every important event in human history. Among these records are the detailed events of September 11, 2001, when the World Trade Center buildings were destroyed. Future catastrophic events that may completely destroy New York City, are also detailed in the code. The possible ramifications of such events are outlined here along with documentation of scientists that tell the same story.

DOOMSDAY NEW YORK

WARNINGS OF DESTRUCTION

Since the early 1980's, I have been using my paintings and writings to sound the warning that New York is the end time Babylon to be destroyed by God, as prophesied in the Bible's book of Revelation or the Apocalypse. In 1999, I wrote a chapter for Mustang Publishing, concerning the Mother of Harlots, in *Wonders to Behold: The Visionary Art of Myrtice West*. A few excerpts follow.

... Revelation 17:18 identifies as "that great city, which reigneth over the kings of the earth." Many biblical scholars see within the harlot a dual prophecy concerning both political and religious fulfillments. In the prophetic fulfillment of **political or secular Babylon, New York**— the original capital of the United States—is the "**great city**." The United Nations is headquartered in New York City. The Greek New

Testament rendering for "reigneth over" is *basileian epi*, meaning "kingdom superimposed." The harlot is the great city "having a kingdom superimposed on the kings of the earth." The troops and policies of the United States and United Nations are superimposed on virtually all the nations and kings of the world. Thus, New York, representing the United States, is that great city which reigns over the kingdoms of the earth.

... the judgment of the Mother of Harlots may be the destruction of New York (and possibly the United States) ...

...a reference to "the waters ...where the whore sitteth," which are "peoples, and multitudes, and nations, and tongues" (Revelation 17:15). "Nations" is rendered here from the Greek *ethnos* (viz., ethnic groups), and "tongues" are languages. (The English language is a conglomeration of many world languages.) Thus, the United States of America is Mystery Babylon, the Great Harlot.

...Tyrus (Ezekiel 27:3-4) and Babylon (Jeremiah 51:13; Rev. 17) are both described as being a great merchant seaport that is represented by a woman situated at the entry of the sea (Statue of Liberty). When the U.S. Babylon is destroyed as prophesied, "the kings of the earth ...shall bewail her" since they will no longer receive gifts, and "the merchants of the earth shall weep and mourn" (Revelation 18:9-11), because they have lost the outlet for their merchandise.

(*Wonders to Behold: The Visionary Art of Myrtice West*, excerpts from chapter 10, "Mother of Harlots," by Norbert H. Kox).

The Revelation description of Babylon Perfectly fits New York as the great import city of the world, that will be destroyed in the last days.

[7] How much she hath glorified herself, and lived deliciously, so much torment and sorrow give her: for she saith in her heart, I sit a queen, and am no widow, and shall see no sorrow.

[8] Therefore shall her plagues come in one day, death, and mourning, and famine; and **she shall be utterly burned with fire**: for strong is Yahweh God who judgeth her.

[9] And the kings of the earth, who have committed fornication and lived deliciously with her, shall bewail her, and lament for her, when **they shall see the smoke of her burning**,

[10] Standing afar off for the fear of her torment, saying, Alas, alas, that great city Babylon, that mighty city! for in one hour is thy judgment come.

[11] And the merchants of the earth shall weep and mourn over her; for no man buyeth their merchandise any more:

[12] The merchandise of gold, and silver, and precious stones, and of pearls, and fine linen, and purple, and silk, and scarlet, and all thyine wood, and all manner vessels of ivory, and all manner vessels of most precious wood, and of brass, and iron, and marble,

[13] And cinnamon, and odours, and ointments, and frankincense, and wine, and oil, and fine flour, and wheat, and beasts, and sheep, and horses, and chariots, and slaves, and souls of men.

[14] And the fruits that thy soul lusted after are departed from thee, and all things which were dainty and goodly are departed from thee, and thou shalt find them no more at all.

[15] The merchants of these things, which were made rich by her, shall stand afar off for the fear of her torment, weeping and wailing,

[16] And saying, Alas, alas, that great city, that was clothed in fine linen, and purple, and scarlet, and

decked with gold, and precious stones, and pearls!

[17] For in one hour so great riches is come to nought. And every shipmaster, and all the company in ships, and sailors, and as many as trade by sea, stood afar off,

[18] And cried when **they saw the smoke of her burning**, saying, What city is like unto this great city!

[19] And they cast dust on their heads, and cried, weeping and wailing, saying, Alas, alas, that great city, wherein were made rich all that had ships in the sea by reason of her costliness! for in one hour is she made desolate.

[20] Rejoice over her, thou heaven, and ye holy apostles and prophets; for God hath avenged you on her.

[21] And a mighty angel took up a stone like a great millstone, and cast it into the sea, saying, Thus **with violence shall that great city Babylon be thrown down**, and shall be found no more at all.

[22] And the voice of harpers, and musicians, and of pipers, and trumpeters, shall be heard no more at all in thee; and no craftsman, of whatsoever craft he be, shall be found any more in thee; and the sound of a millstone shall be heard no more at all in thee;

[23] And the light of a candle shall shine no more at all in thee; and the voice of the bridegroom and of the bride shall be heard no more at all in thee: for thy merchants were the great men of the earth; for by thy sorceries were all nations deceived.

(Revelation 18: 7-23).

When the World Trade Center buildings were disintegrated on September 11, 2001, it definitely looked like the beginning of the end. As I watched the television screen with horror, my eyes drifted over a few inches to a picture I had painted of the towers being destroyed. As my eyes danced back and forth between the television and the painting a nausea erupted in the pit of my stomach. When the towers fell on live television, my first thoughts were, "This looks like the controlled demolitions I've seen in the past. I have seen buildings demolished, and they fall straight down, just like this." It was sheer horror and astonishment.

THIS DRY ROOT

This Dry Root: *As this root is plucked from the ground, so shall your heart be plucked from the midst of you*, 1/28/01, digital collage and acrylic

Following is a portion of a letter I wrote two weeks later explaining the prophetic episode.

The Trade Tower piece shown here is something I *completed* in Bimini, January 28, 2001 (**eight months before the 911 disaster**). The title is "This Dry Root." The theme is, "As this root is plucked from the ground, so shall your heart be plucked from the midst of you."

The morning of 9/11/01, when I turned on the TV and saw all the smoke rising from Manhattan, I almost fell over. Her heart was plucked from the midst of her.

(Portion of letter to *Art Visionary*, 1/31/02).

When I had received the **inspiration for this painting, in December of 2000**, there was a certain horror that overcame me as I looked at the picture of the towers. I trembled. There was a knowledge that the towers would fall. I did not know how it would happen, but I knew without doubt that the heart of Babylon was about to be plucked violently from her midst. *Nine months later the towers went down. (This Dry Root* was not exhibited publicly, but was viewed in the studio, on several occasions between December 2000 through January 2001, by the crew and passengers of Blackbeard Cruises, on their frequent visits to the Island of Bimini).

I had previously sent out the warning in 1998 with my *Apocalypse to Eternity* 4-panel installation-painting (14 feet high and 60 feet wide) at the *South Bend Indiana Regional Art Museum (Walls Talk*, November 1998). The same piece was Abbreviated to 9 feet high by 30 feet wide, and displayed at *The End is Near* exhibit in New York in 1999. This abbreviated form was exhibited at The Las Vegas Art Museum also in 1999. In 2000 it was shown at the Dean Jensen Gallery, Milwaukee. It was exhibited for the fifth time in 2000-2001, in a special exhibit titled, "The End is a New Beginning," at Lehigh University, Bethlehem,

Pennsylvania.

When the piece first showed in 1998, it scared me. I could see fire coming down on New York. I wanted to believe it was symbolic, but had an awful feeling that it was all too real. It was awesome and frightening to know. As I stood there during the opening I wanted to cry aloud and sound the alarm, "Get out of New York!" But the inner voice said, "Keep silent. Let the paintings speak. He who has ears will hear."

In 1999, my painting titled "Bimini" (4 ft. x 18 ft.) attracted the rage of the Catholic League of New York. More than 40 Green Bay members marched the picket lines in front of the Neville Public Museum during my three-month exhibit, "To Hell and Back." Several images offended them. They failed to look beneath the surface and completely missed the message.

The *Bimini* painting is inundated with Bible Codes. These codes are for the viewer, especially the Hebrew speaking viewer, since the codes are written in Hebrew. In this painting the main code matrix issues a warning to the United States, which refers to the two towers falling and burning as a furnace. I didn't realize the *towers* referred to the Trade Towers, until after September 11, but I did know that it involved New York.

In the 1999 book, *Wonders to Behold: the Visionary Art of Myrtice West,* I wrote the chapter, "Mother of Harlots" (pp. 114-120) issuing the warning to New York and the United States loud and clear.

My 1996 painting, "Mother of Harlots: the Pie-eyed Piper" (*ibid*. p.120) shows the Trade Center buildings exploding and burning. The beast with ten horns hates the woman (the great city) and burns her with fire (Revelation 17: 16-18). In the painting the claws of the great beast are seen piercing and exploding the towers at the point where the 9-11 terrorist planes would eventually initiate their destruction.

Did I have a special vision? No. I studied the Bible, deciphered the code, and painted intuitively.

Mother of Harlots: the Pie-eyed Piper, 1996, acrylic & oil

Since 1984, and earlier, I have sounded the warnings in my writings, and since 1989, in my paintings. But in 1998, it became more urgent, unavoidable and undeniable.

I wish I could believe that the fulfillment of the prophecies were satisfied on September 11, 2001. But I am afraid that they were not. There is more to come.

The prophecies of the book of Revelation (*The Apocalypse*) clearly fit the scene of 9-11. Then doesn't it make sense to expect the rest of the prophecies to follow? If so, we can expect suffering such as this earth has never before seen. And we will be right in the midst of it.

I will put together a list of Scriptures and codes that will show you without a doubt that what I have said is true, and that these are not my words, but ancient prophecies written before they happened, the end of time proclaimed from the beginning.

(Portion of letter to *Art Visionary*, 1/31/02).

911 ATTACK FORESEEN

Ezekiel prophesied the "watchman," and he prophesied the inevitable end that is to come upon the United States, as well as the destruction of the World Trade Center towers that took place September 11, 2001.

The United States is cryptically referred to by Ezekiel. Abbreviated, ארהב, the United States appears in a three-skip ELS, in Ezekiel 7:5. It is spelled out by the first letters of each Hebrew word in the phrase, "***an only evil, behold, it is come***," אחת רעה הנה באה (plain text Hebrew reads from right to left). There it is, ארהב, the United States (Manasseh/Israel).

Also, thou son of man, thus saith the Lord Yahweh unto the land of Israel; An end, the end is come upon the four corners of the land.

Now is the end come upon thee, and I will send mine anger upon thee, and will judge thee according to thy ways, and will recompense upon thee all thine abominations.

And mine eye shall not spare thee, neither will I have pity: but I will recompense thy ways upon thee, and thine abominations shall be in the midst of thee: and ye shall know that I am Yahweh.

Thus saith the Lord Yahweh; An evil, **an only evil, behold, it is come** [אֶ֣חָ֣ד הָ֣רָ֣ע = USA, 3-skip].

An end is come, the end is come: it watcheth for thee; behold, it is come.

The *cycle-of-time* (circling: צְפִירָה) is come unto thee, O thou that dwellest in the land: the time is come, **the day of trouble is near**, and not the sounding again of the mountains.

Now will I shortly pour out my fury upon thee, and accomplish mine anger upon thee: and I will judge thee according to thy ways, and will recompense thee for all thine abominations.

And mine eye shall not spare, neither will I have pity: I will recompense thee according to thy ways and thine abominations that are in the midst of thee; and **ye shall know that I am Yahweh that *strikes***.

(Ezekiel 7:2-9).

Most Americans do not want to admit God's judgment in 911. They refuse to see it as a punishment, and repent. This does not mean the people who lost their lives in the towers were any worse than anyone else, but that America as a whole needs to repent. Throughout Bible history God has employed evil nations to chastise the stiff-necked and proud Israelites. Evil terrorists can still be used as an instrument by God to chastise his straying people in the last days. **We are the Israelites** (at this late time the lost tribes have without a doubt mixed to include a certain portion of people of all nationalities and races).

When God executes his purpose he tells us to take note that he declared it before it happened.

Remember the former things of old: for I am God, and there is none else; I am God, and there is none like me,

Declaring the end from the beginning, and from ancient times the things that are not yet done, saying, My counsel shall stand, and I will do all my pleasure:

Calling a ravenous bird from the east, the man that executeth my counsel from a far country: yea, I have spoken it, I will also bring it to pass; I have purposed it, I will also do it.

(Isaiah 46:**9-11**).

These verses seem to apply to **9-11**. The airplanes could be ravenous birds flown by terrorists from a far country in the East. This does not imply that Bin Ladin was a holy man. It simply means God can enlist whomever he wishes to initiate his judgment. Yahweh has done this before when his people strayed.

The section of Isaiah under scrutiny holds hidden messages in an elaborate symmetrical matrix (ELS 130-skip; Isaiah 44:19 through 51:23) encoding in great detail the events of 911 (this was partially **shown, 2 1/2 years before 911**, in my 1999 epic painting titled "Bimini").

Bimini (detail) acrylic on canvas, 1999, displaying symmetrical Bible Code

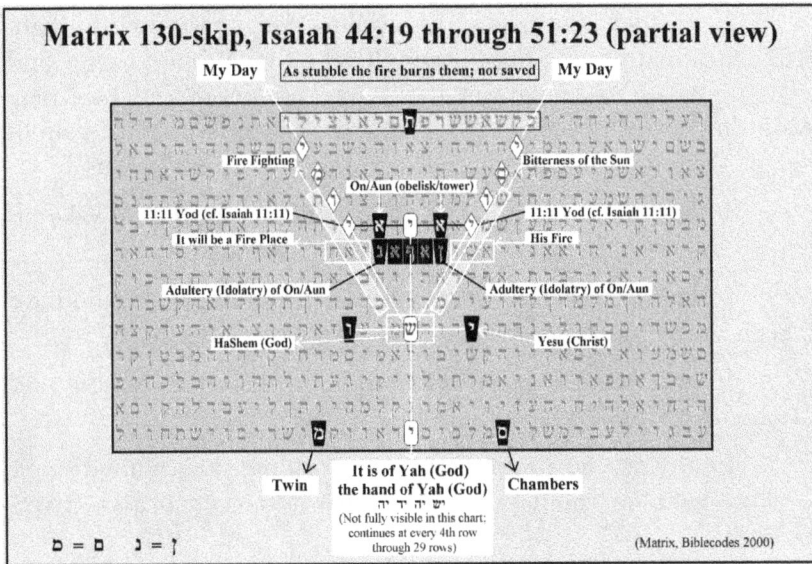

Matrix 130-skip, Isaiah 44:19 through 51:23 (partial view)

Partial elaboration on the symmetrical grid from the 1999 *Bimini* painting

In this Isaiah grid the words "twin" and "chambers," intersected by the double appearance of the word On/Aun signify the Twin Towers; and "it will be as a fireplace." The dual term "My day" rises symmetrically from the letter *Shin* in the middle of Yesu and HaShem; *Shin* is the mother letter symbolizing fire. The same *Shin* is crossed by the phrase, "It is [existence/substance] of Yah, the hand of Yah," indicating the fire was God's judgment. "As stubble the fire burns them; not saved," is the portion of the surface text of Isaiah 47:14 that falls here symmetrically at the top of this chart, and the phrase "Declaring the bitterness of my fire," also appears symmetrically, higher up in the expanded matrix (Isaiah 46:10).

The word On (אן also אן) connects Manasseh to the U.S. (Genesis 41:45-52) seen twice vertically, *viz.* the standing towers, and twice horizontally, the two fallen towers. AUN, spelled with the vowel letter, has the alternate meanings "wealth" and "wickedness."

The tragedy of 911 brought no humility to the American people. Our country just will not repent. Briefly it looked like they might. For the first few nights after the attack even the night time talk show hosts were very sober. There was none of their usual filthy humor, only straight talk. That may have lasted a week and things got back to their normal obscenities. They were only temporarily silent from shock.

It was not long before the swelling American pride brought forth proclamations aiming for new heights: We'll build bigger and better, the tallest towers anyone in this world has ever seen. God may knock down our towers of Babel, first one, then two, but it cannot stop us. We'll just build again; as if taunting, "You can't stop us."

Why can't we be humble? We should accept it as a wake-up call. If God used this to get our attention it is for a reason.

Instead of reacting with violence and pride, we should have all been sitting in the dust crying out to God for guidance.

In a television special about 911, people were cursing and blaspheming God just like the Bible said they would.

One Catholic priest said, "God couldn't be counted upon like I thought he could. At ground zero it seemed like God was absent."

A rabbi said, "How can you say it was God's plan that someone made it out and another did not."

Several people said they hate God now. One man said he hates God and curses and damns God for 911, and that he will never forgive God.

It is very sad that people got killed. But when things like this happen maybe it is to get our attention, to make us think, and to cause us to be better people as a result. One time Yesu taught a lesson by referencing a much smaller tower disaster, as an example to call people unto repentance, when he said, "Those eighteen, upon whom the tower in Siloam fell, and slew them, think ye that they were sinners above all men that dwelt in Jerusalem? I tell you, Nay: but, except ye repent, ye shall all likewise perish." (Luke 13:4-5).

Those three thousand on whom the trade towers fell were very unfortunate to be there at that time. It does not mean they were evil. But when we can understand that **those towers fell because it was prophesied**, we should start looking at the big picture. We are into something very serious here, where **every move is known ahead of time**.

911 WAS THE FULFILLMENT OF A CURSE

Psalm 23:4, says, **"I am walking in the valley of the shadow of death. I will not fear evil."** The Hebrew text is,

אלך בגיא צלמות לא אירא רע. Counting every second letter, (a 2-skip ELS) gives us, ארר אלול רג [כג. *sof*, ך=כ]. The transcription of this phrase is, "Elul 23 curse." In 2001, Elul 23, is September 11. Translated into English this code reads, **"September 11 Curse."**

The **911** tragedy was a curse. Daniel **9:11**, says the **curse** is poured out upon us for transgression of the Torah (law); and Revelation **9:11** tells us Abaddon, aka Apollyon (Destruction/ Destroyer) is the king of the bottomless **pit** (cf. Isaiah 14:12-15).

Reporters referred to the 911 ground-zero as the **pit.**

911 WAS A NATIONAL PUNISHMENT

Both the surface text and the symmetrical ELS codes of Ezekiel 7, suggest that 911 was a divine punishment.

The towers were symbolic and had to fall like the original Tower of Babel fell. First one, then two, "Give unto her double." This is not a pronouncement of condemnation on all those who died in the attack. It is a judgment on the people of the USA in general, not individuals. It is sad that sometimes innocent people are in the wrong place at the wrong time and end up suffering or dying as a result of it. Because our nation's populous, including religious people, have strayed far from God, we are being shaken to our roots. This nation has reached the height of corruption and is about to collapse. According to Scripture Yahweh is chastising his people to get their attention, because he is calling his remnant together from the far reaches of the Earth and from the islands of the seas. The lost tribes of Israel (many are Christians) in the United States and Great Britain are soon to be reunited with the remnant of true Jews who comprise the nation Judah. Much suffering will happen in the process. We are about to be jolted like never before as the powers of heaven unite with the forces of nature to shake this Earth like a drunken man.

...Because America has chosen the wrong road, tribulation has already begun. When disaster hit New York in 2001, when the Twin Towers fell, this was an act of God. There was no way anyone could have intervened to stop it. People always want to put the blame on someone else, instead of taking the blame themselves. No one individual is to blame, it's American citizens who are to blame for their rejecting God's laws.

Another act of God is going to take place in the future, which will cost millions of lives. The "Big Apple" (New York) will be destroyed. This disaster will weaken this nation, then sorrow and tribulation will increase across America.

(p. 206, *America in Prophecy and the Apocalypse*).

MORE JUDGMENT TO COME

Examine the following charts to see how 911, and the coming ferocious onslaught of nature, were predicted and encoded into the Scriptures thousands of years ago, even with the accurate names of New York, the United States and more.

The code matrix we are examining is the one where New York appears at a 15-skip ELS. This causes the Bible text to be laid out in lines with 15 letters in each line. Portions of the same 15-letter grid will be shown multiple times, to allow for the orderly display of the numerous terms, without too much overlapping. Otherwise, if all the terms were displayed in one chart they would overlap and obliterate each other. Practically every letter in the grid would be marked, making it impossible to read.

In Hebrew, when a string of letters is read, it can often have several meanings, because depending where you divide it, different words may be present. In other words, several sentences could be made up of the exact same sequence of letters.

Our search term, New York appears in several sentences this way: 1. **New York Fear is pandemic**; 2. **New York is fearing decay of splendor**; 3. **New York is fearing the circle** (surrounding).

At the top of the matrix a wheel of symmetrical letters and words spell out the times we are living in, "**Time of evil; Evil time**."

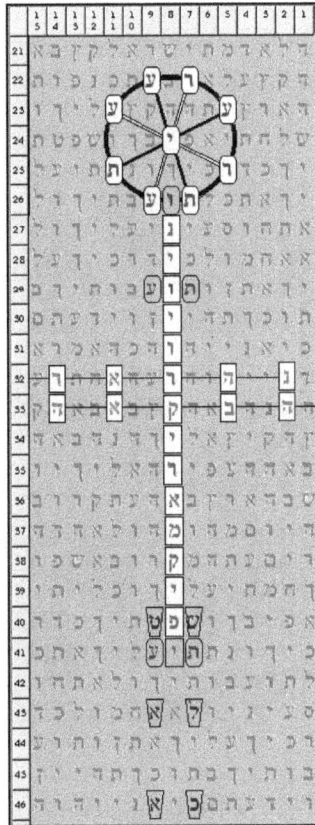

New York
Ezekiel 7:2-9 Matrix
15 Skip

Time of evil

Evil time

← The river/flow of the United States is vomit

↓

"New York fear is pandemic"

Bible Codes 2000

Where the United States appears in a three-skip ELS, in Ezekiel 7:5, the entire encoded ten-character phrase in the symmetrical matrix grid says, "The river/flow of the United States is vomit." This evidently refers to the corruption oozing from the U.S. in this time of evil.

New York

Ezekiel 7:2-9 Matrix
15 Skip

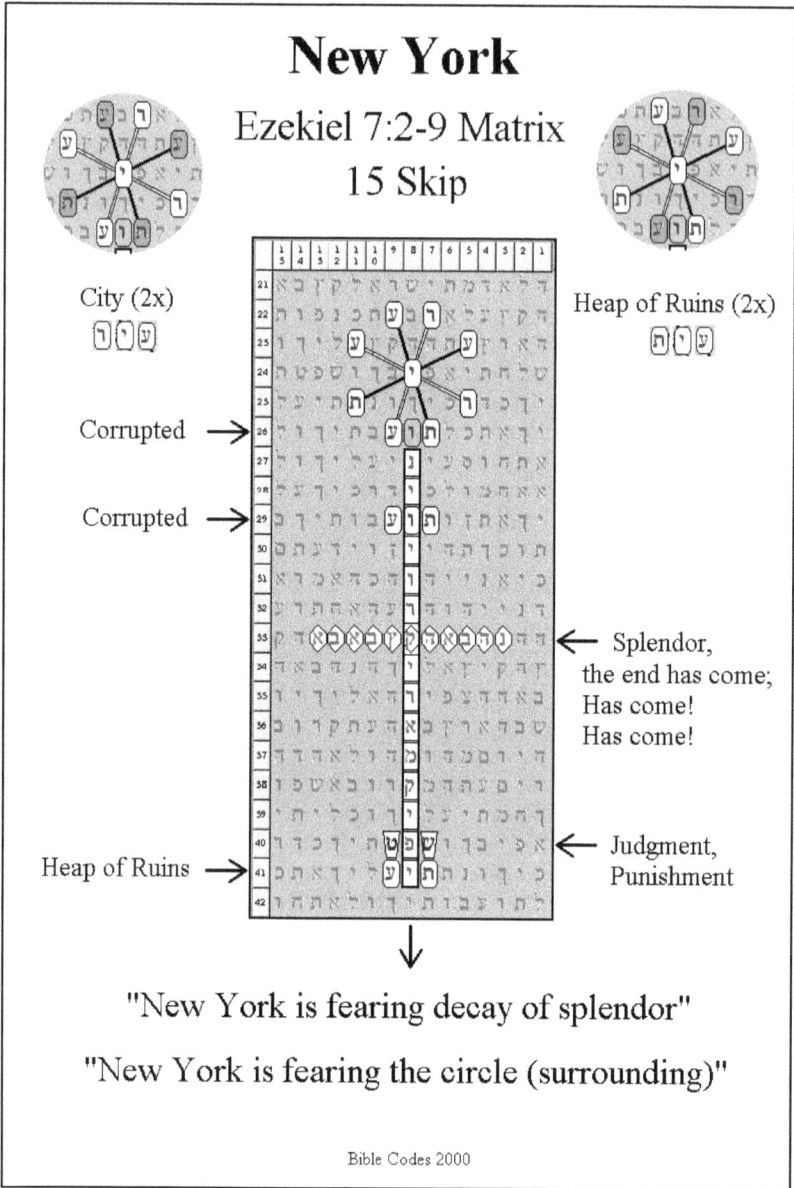

City (2x)

Heap of Ruins (2x)

Corrupted →

Corrupted →

Heap of Ruins →

← Splendor,
the end has come;
Has come!
Has come!

← Judgment,
Punishment

↓

"New York is fearing decay of splendor"

"New York is fearing the circle (surrounding)"

Bible Codes 2000

The word "corrupted," comes up symmetrically several times in the grid.

The pin-wheel array at the top of the matrix shows "city" and "heap of ruins," overlapped as a double-cross.

It is a very interesting "coincidence," based on the laws of synchronicity, that these very terms, **city** and **heap of ruins**, which appear twice, criss-crossed in the Ezekiel/New York grid, also appear connected to 911, in the *Complete Word Study Dictionary of the New Testament.*

> *New Testament Dictionary* includes the following phrases on page **911**: "unawares; hewn in rock; community of free people, disorganized crowd or multitude; a rich, commercial city; the Muslims destroyed **the city**, and today it is a **heap of ruins**."
>
> (p. 911, Zodhiates, Spiros; *Complete Word Study Dictionary: New Testament* ["911 (Sept. 11) in Alphabetics—Prophecy of Day of Distress," *http://www.greaterthings.com*).

Seen at the top of the Ezekiel grid (in a subsequent chart) "*The end, on high: four wings*," tells us it is destruction from the heights, by four wings. An airplane has two wings. Two planes have "four wings." The towers were struck by two planes. An alternate translation is, "***The end, on high: a timed ambush, of wings***." The planes (*wings*) were hijacked (*ambushed*) and used for a "timed" ambush to destroy the towers, "the end on high."

New York
Ezekiel 7:2-9 Matrix
15 Skip

The end, on high: Four wings

Passed away (reversed)

For terror, shall be my anger on you, and judgment

Heap of Ruins

Corrupted

To crush you

Corrupted

Splendor, the end has come; Has come! Has come!

Woe! Woe!

Judgment, Punishment

Heap of Ruins

Corrupted — City

"New York is fearing decay of splendor"

"New York is fearing the circle (surrounding)"

Bible Codes 2000

The word "corrupted," crosses directly through the w in New York. Two *woes* form an X, encoded symmetrically through, the intersection of *corrupted New York*, indicating the "double judgment," that has been prophesied against this nation.

New York
Ezekiel 7:2-9 Matrix
15 Skip

← The day of panic and of sympathy

To become fat; foolish; dull →

← Judgment; Punishment

↓ ↓

911 Thrown down

"New York fear is pandemic"

(central vertical key-term, alternate translation)

Bible Codes 2000

This Hebrew word for Judgment, in reverse, means to become fat, foolish, or dull. It tells us why we are being judged, because we have become fat and dull. This country has grave spiritual and moral problems. Our fatness, easy living, has put the ways of God on the back burner. The so-called freedom of this country has virtually destroyed morality. The U. S. A. thinks of itself as the great "I Am," beyond judgment (Isaiah 47:7-10, cf, Revelation 18:6-8).

From the first and last letters of the word "judgment," are the symmetrically encoded terms, "911" and "thrown down," confirming that it was not just a terrorist attack, but an actual chastisement from God, to get our attention, because we had grown "fat" and become "dull."

Scripture says, "...Thus **with violence shall that great city Babylon be thrown down** ..." (Revelation 18:21).

The terms "911" and "thrown down" stand vertically, side-by-side in the matrix, like the twin towers they represent.

These findings are so astounding you might want to verify them yourself. If you do not have a computer and the proper equipment and knowledge, you can work out this grid by hand. Just get a Hebrew Tanach (Bible) and a piece of graph paper. Copy the Hebrew letters from Ezekiel 7, in rows of 15 letters per line, with the first letter in the same place as in this grid. You will create this same matrix. Then get out your Hebrew dictionaries and start checking words. This is how I first found the Ezekiel 7 code, in 1997, before I even knew how to use a computer.

During *The End Is Near* exhibition at American Visionary Art Museum, in 1997, I met Apocalyptic Artist Frank Bruno, who has become a close friend. He introduced me to the Bible Code at that time, with several articles and books. The material was so extraordinary that I had to check it for accuracy. I got out my Hebrew Bible and began counting the Equidistant Letter Sequences by hand. What they said was true. The codes did exist.

Having confirmed the validity of hidden codes, I began researching portions of Scripture that were apparently key passages. Ezekiel 7, speaks of the end, and judgment in the surface text. Verses 3-4, are worded the same as 8-9, indicating double judgment. It correlates to the United States. Previous studies had shown New York to represent the U.S. as end-time Babylon. She receives double judgment (Revelation 18:2-8).

In the section between these identical judgment verses, I discovered New York at a 15-skip ELS. Then I prepared a graph with fifteen letters per line and New York fell in the central vertical column. I had already found clues to the importance of symmetry encoded in the book of Genesis. So, I searched the grid like a word puzzle looking for related interlocking words in a symmetrical pattern within the matrix.

These findings inspired the colossal 1998 painting, *Apocalypse to Eternity*, depicting the *double-destruction* of New York.

Apocalypse to Eternity, detail panel, "Death of Babylon: Double Destruction"

Decay of Splendour, 2003, acrylic, by N. H. Kox (Henry Boxer Gallery, London)

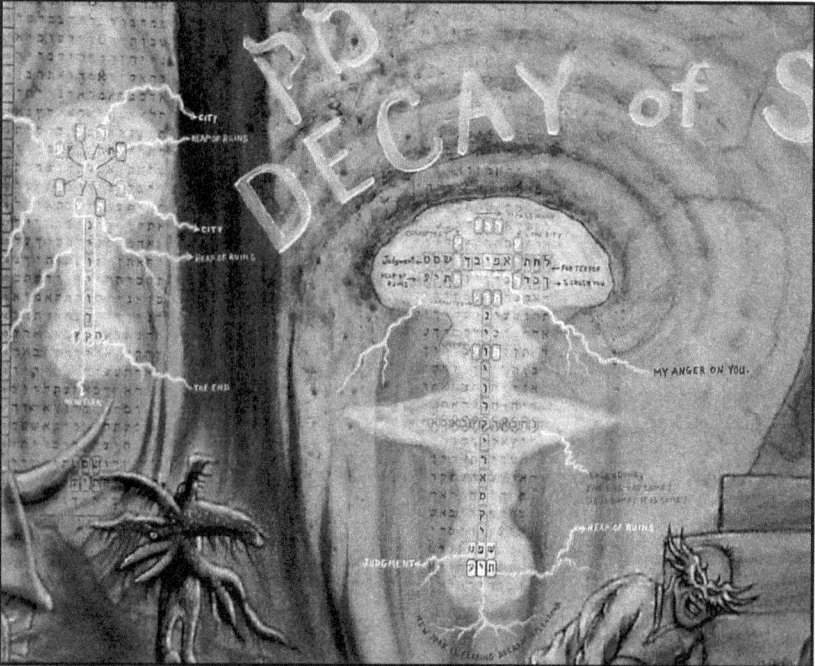

Decay of Splendour (detail)

The *Decay of Splendour* painting developed from a scene at the base of the Statue of Liberty, in *Apocalypse to Eternity*, and incorporates the Ezekiel 7, New York matrix grid.

Decay of Splendour (detail)

In the details of *Decay of Splendour*, you can see the amazing array of related terms in a symmetrical pattern, within the Ezekiel 7/New York grid. The order of these letters in Scripture was

48

determined thousands of years ago, when there was no New York to even think about.

These complex encryptions were not designed by a human mind. The concept of New York and the events encoded here, could only have been known by an omnipresent eternal being, free from the constraints of time and space. It seems apparent this would be Yahweh/Yesu, the Creator.

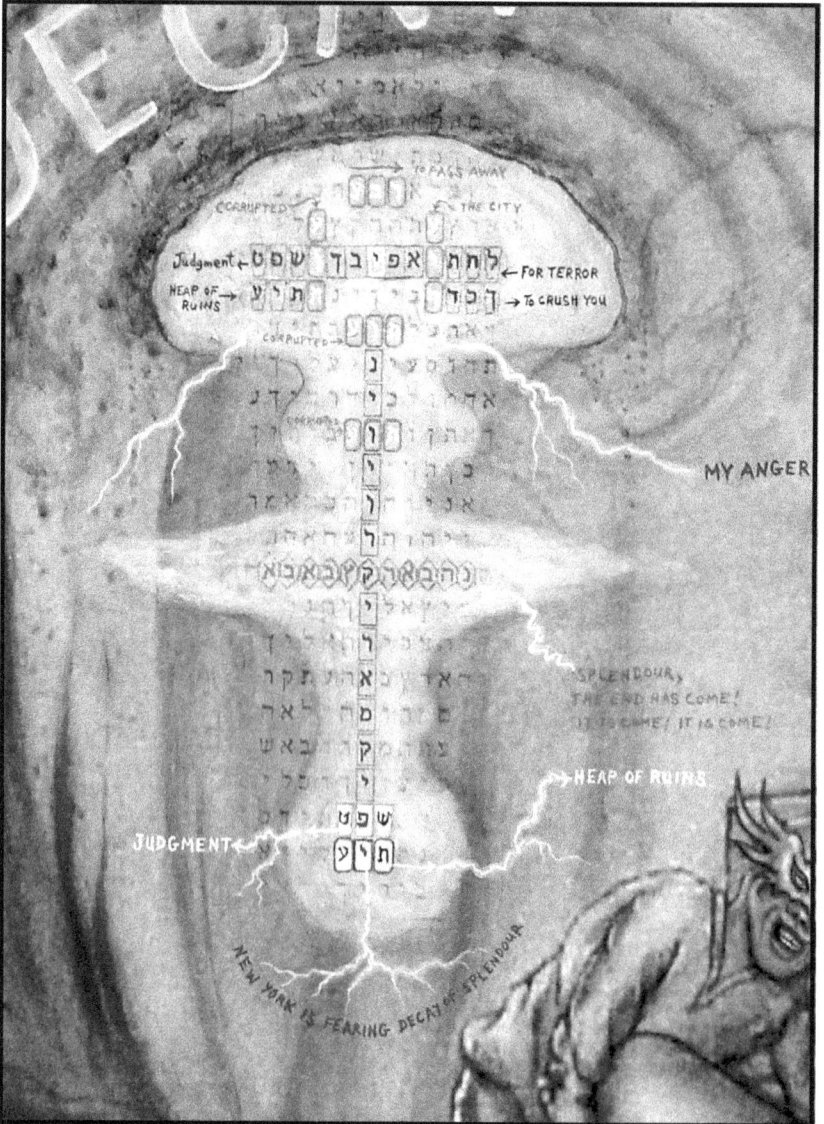

Decay of Splendour (detail)

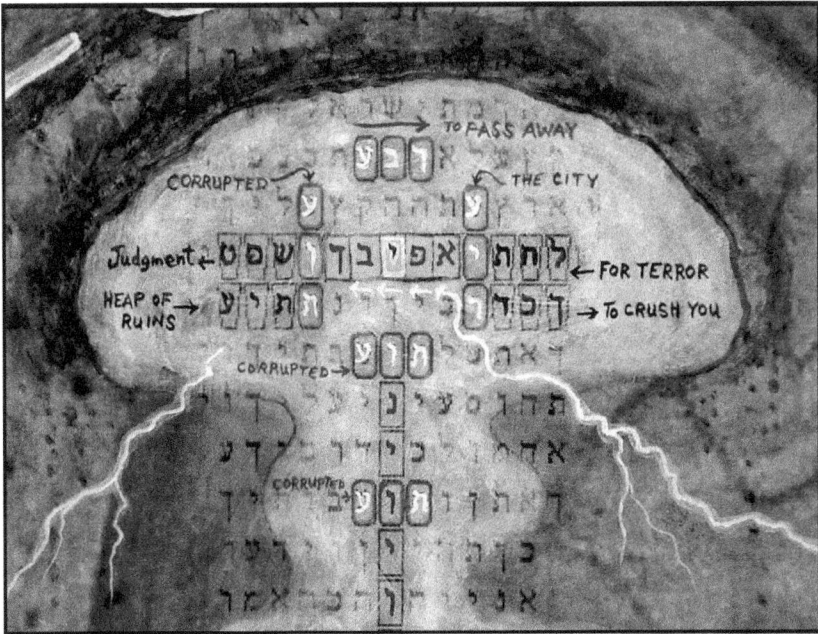

Decay of Splendour (detail)

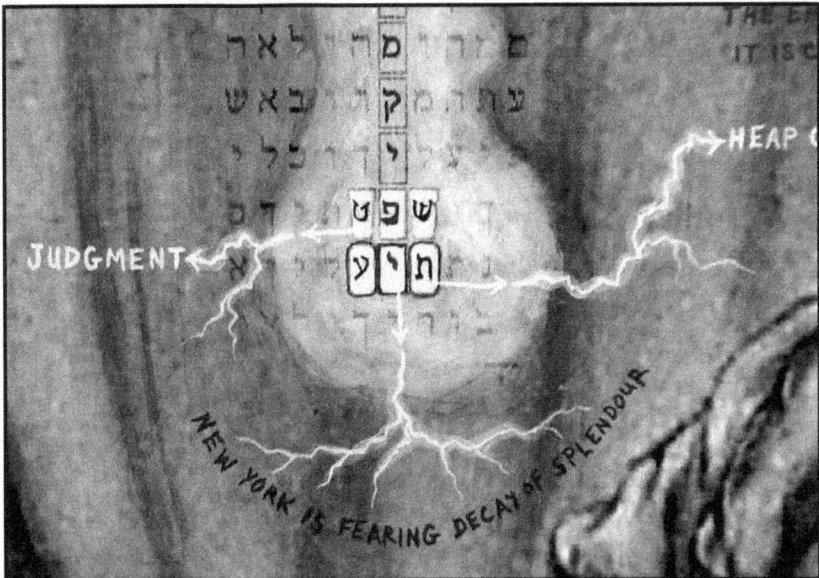

Decay of Splendour (detail)

Many of the search terms were found in 1997, when the grid was first revealed. Others were discovered during the writing of this text (2006) while re-examining the matrix.

"*The end, on high: four wings,*" "*The end, on high: a timed ambush, of wings,*" "911" and "thrown down," are clear ties to the attack on the World Trade Center.

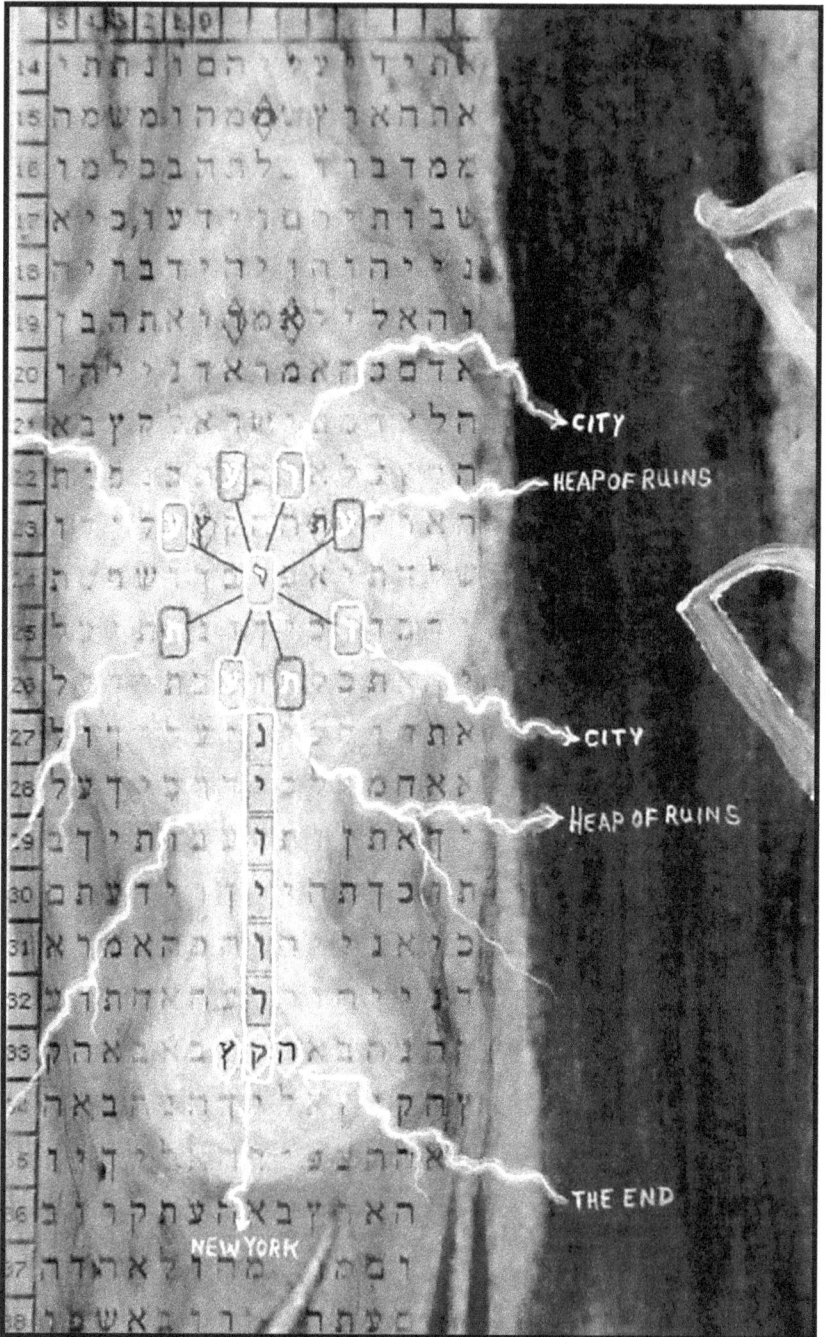

Decay of Splendour (detail)

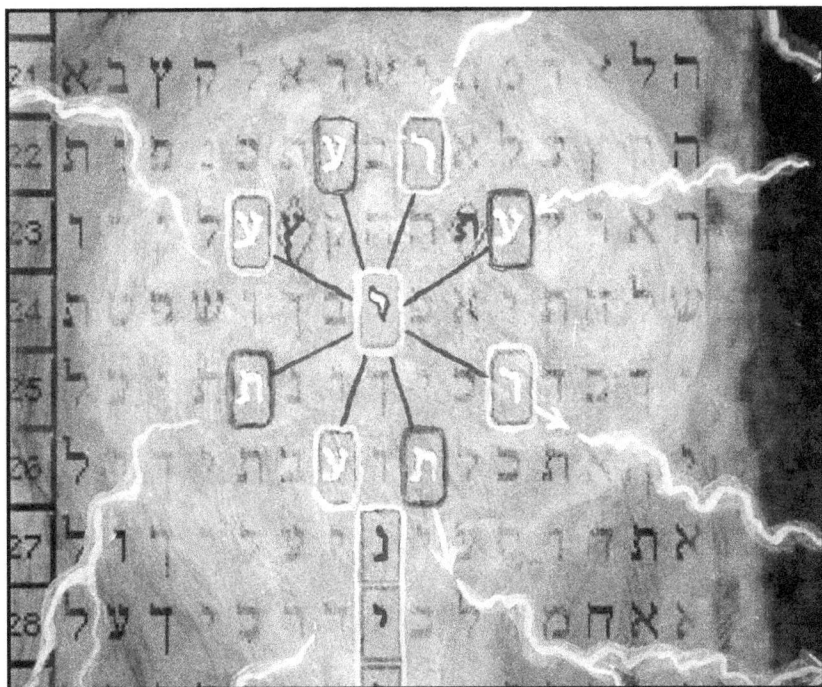

Decay of Splendour (detail)

CONEY ISLAND

In this New York grid the terms "city" and "heap of ruins," each appear twice, criss-crossed on their central *yod*, like the hub of a Ferris Wheel. The image it creates literally suggests a carnival setting, and brings to mind the phrase "Playground of the World," which has been designated to New York's Coney Island, ever since the 1800's. This prompted me to search for Coney Island within the grid. The word "Coney," appears twice.

In its first appearance it superimposes the name New York and stands as the shaft supporting the Ferris Wheel (see following matrix chart). Coney Island is New York's carnival amusement park, and here the word Coney completes the image of the Ferris Wheel. It appears a second time just to the right in another ELS, as an additional confirmation.

To the untrained eye, it may look like two different spellings. This is due to the initial and final (*sof*) forms of the

New York
Ezekiel 7:2-6 Matrix
15 Skip

(Coney Island)

Coney

Coney

Window of God

Window of
lamenting/wailing

The word "Coney" superimposed
on top of New York

Coney = כוני = כו נ י = Window of N.Y.

ניו יורק = New York

נ י = N.Y.

ני = lamenting, wailing

ך & כ = Kaph = K or C (k-sound, as in Coney)

ן & נ = Nun = N

Bible Codes 2000

letters *Kaph* כ/ך (c with k-sound) and *Nun* נ/ן (n), as found in the Hebrew text. Coney is spelled כוני. It appears in this grid as כוני and ךונ. This is simply due to the appearance of the *sof* letters which are treated the same as initial letters in the codes.

If we split the word Coney in half, the Hebrew letters spell "window of lamenting," or, "window of wailing." The *nun-yod* are N and Y, so, it could also be "window of N.Y. (New York)."

My attention has been called to the fact that there was an elegant restaurant called "Windows on the World," on the 107th floor of the World Trade Center's north tower. This was a "Window of New York," and truly became a window of wailing and lamenting on September 11, 2001.

Where we see the ELS, "window of lamenting/wailing," on the right, symmetrically to the left we find "window of God," suggesting that the window may represent some type of portal between the spiritual and physical realms. It may also be a window of destruction, or it may be a window of repentance that Yahweh is allowing us for change.

WARNING FOR THOSE WATCHING

The Hebrew letter cluster in "Coney" represents another significant phrase, with various implications. The first three letters can be translated *established* or *appointed*. The final *yod*, as a suffix, means *my*. So it could read, "my established" or "my appointed." This may be God's confirmation that the code and prophecies are established and appointed by him.

The same word means *faithful and steadfast*. So it could read, "my faithful," or "my steadfast." This seems to indicate that he is communicating this message to his faithful.

It can also mean "to be set," "to be ready," "be prepared." God is telling us to be ready for something. He is warning us so that we can prepare for what is coming upon us. He is giving us a chance to be ready. **He is making a way for some to escape**.

"But they that escape of them shall escape, and shall be on the mountains like doves of the valleys, all of them mourning, every one for his iniquity." (Ezekiel 7:16).

It sounds like the "window of wailing." Those who escape will be mourning for their iniquity and wailing for themselves, but there are many who do not escape. For them there is no wailing. "Violence is risen up into a rod of wickedness: none of them shall remain, nor of their multitude, nor of any of theirs: neither shall there be wailing for them." (Ezekiel 7:11).

This portion of Scripture reveals intricate details in the Code, and even the surface text perfectly aligns with its hidden messages.

NEXT DISASTER FOR NEW YORK

Over the years, Coney Island has actually become connected to Long Island, the main land mass of New York. A search for Long Island, in the Ezekiel 7, New York grid, reveals the diagonal phrase, **"Long Island is crushed/pounded."** Crossing it symmetrically and forming an X over New York, is the word cluster **"It shall be divided/cut; It shall be so."** (see matrix chart).

At the base of the X, is the phrase, "The cycle-of-time (circle) is of God," *i.e.*, "The cycle-of-time is God's."

If we read these phrases together, along with the central key-sentence, it says, *"New York, fear is pandemic. Long Island is crushed/pounded. It shall be divided/cut; It shall be so. The cycle-of-time is God's."*

This looks like a warning to us from Yahweh. It outlines a judgment in the cycle. Something that evidently has to happen in God's timing. Since this code matrix has so accurately recorded the 911 terrorist attack, we had better take notice and pay attention to its other messages.

Why are we being warned? You would not believe that 911 was the Judgment of Yahweh. If you were not warned ahead of time that Judgment is coming, you would not believe this approaching disaster is Yahweh's judgment. But now you are warned and when it happens you will remember that it was prophesied and it is Divine retribution, and you will know that it was recorded before time.

New York

Ezekiel 7:2-9 Matrix
15 Skip

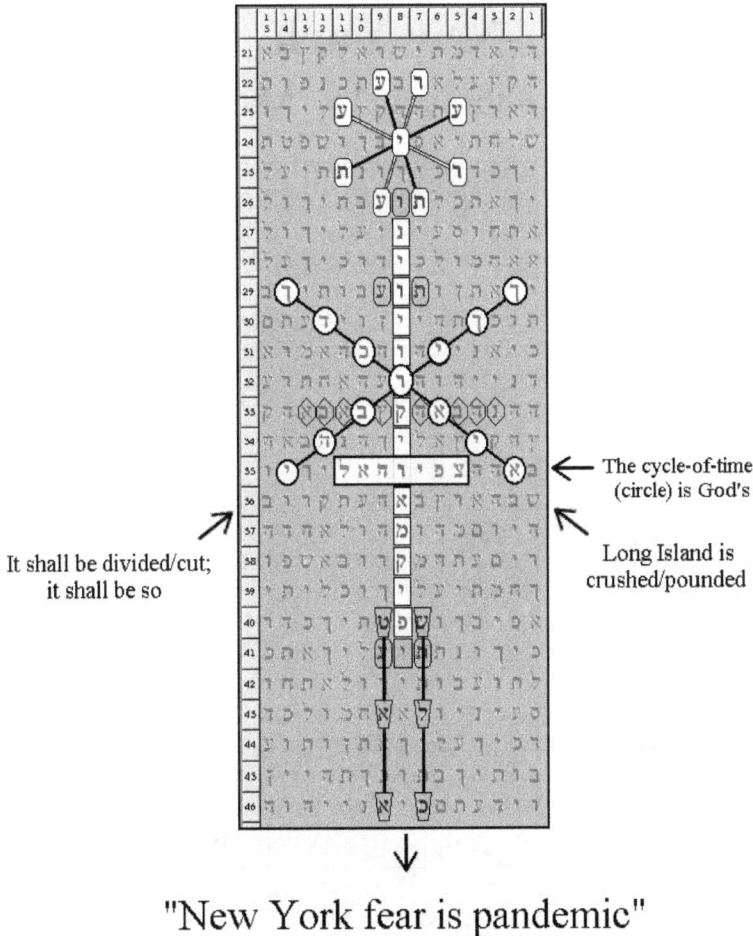

→ The cycle-of-time (circle) is God's

It shall be divided/cut; it shall be so

Long Island is crushed/pounded

"New York fear is pandemic"

Bible Codes 2000

Judgment is coming because we have failed to live by God's plan. In striving to present "freedom" to everyone, the U.S. has corrupted God's Word, his rules and his name. As individuals you can change, but as a whole, it is probably too late for this nation.

In the plain text of the Scripture grid that we are scrutinizing, Yahweh repeats twice, "mine eye shall not spare, neither will I have pity: I will recompense thee according to thy ways and thine abominations that are in the midst of thee; and ye shall know that I am Yahweh that smiteth." (Ezekiel 7:4 & 9).

New York
Ezekiel 6:13 through 7:8   Matrix   15 Skip

Ezekiel 6:13-14 ← ← The Nations (Goyim) are wailing

Evil time

Time of evil

← The river/flow of the United States is vomit

Bible Codes 2000

He gives the warning so the few who will be spared can escape, but also, so that when the rest of the world sees the destruction he brings, they will know that it is "Yahweh that smiteth." All the world will see the awesome and frightening judgment of Yahweh.

New York is the heart of the U.S. and represents the entire country. As such, the warning is to all of us, not just New York. **"The river/flow of the United States is vomit."** But for now, let us concentrate specifically on New York, since we have such precise terms as Long Island, Coney Island and the name of New York, with accurate 911 references.

CRUSHED, POUNDED, DIVIDED AND CUT

What could *crush* and *pound* Long Island until it is *divided* or *cut* in two? What are the implications and ramifications of this prophecy? You probably already have a picture in your mind of a plausible scenario. Let's consider some possibilities.

Is it a literal or a symbolic pounding and dividing? If it were symbolic it might be a crushing or humbling of the people, and a dividing of believers and unbelievers. Scripture says, "What is this then that is written, The stone which the builders rejected, the same is become the head of the corner? Whosoever shall fall upon that stone shall be broken; but on whomsoever it shall fall, it will grind him to powder." (Luke 20:17-18).

But it is more likely a literal crushing and dividing. The code grid revealed the literal destruction of the Trade Towers, in detail, therefore the crushing and dividing of Long Island is probably literal as well.

The towers were taken down by terrorists and Long Island could be destroyed by terrorists too. Although this could happen, another possibility is that of *natural* disaster. An earthquake could literally split the island. Another likely scenario would be a rampant hurricane of super-storm velocity that would pound its way through the island. Perhaps both.

Chapter 27, of Ezekiel, perfectly describes New York as Tyre, which coincides with the symbolic end time Babylon to be broken by the sea:

> And say unto Tyrus, **O thou that art situate at the entry of the sea**, which art a merchant of the people for many isles, Thus saith the Lord Yahweh; O Tyrus, thou hast said, I am of perfect beauty.
>
> Thy borders are in the midst of the seas, thy builders have perfected thy beauty.
> (Ezekiel 27:3-4)
>
> Thy riches, and thy fairs, thy merchandise, thy mariners, and thy pilots, thy calkers, and the occupiers of thy merchandise, and all thy men of war, that are in thee, and in all thy company which is in the midst of thee, **shall fall into the midst of the seas in the day of thy ruin**.
>
> The suburbs shall shake at the sound of the cry of thy pilots.
> (Ezekiel 27:27-28)
>
> In the time when **thou shalt be broken by the seas in the depths of the waters** thy merchandise and all thy company in the midst of thee shall fall.
>
> All the inhabitants of the isles shall be astonished at thee, and their kings shall be sore afraid, they shall be troubled in their countenance.
>
> The merchants among the people shall hiss at thee; thou shalt be a terror, and never shalt be any more.
> (Ezekiel 27:34-36)

The New Testament says, "And there shall be signs in the sun, and in the moon, and in the stars; and upon the earth distress of nations, with perplexity; **the sea and the waves roaring; Men's hearts failing them for fear**, and for looking after those things which are coming on the earth: for the powers of heaven shall be shaken." (Luke 21:25-26).

The Ezekiel 7 symmetrical code says, *"New York, fear is pandemic. Long Island is crushed/pounded. It shall be divided/cut; It shall be so. The cycle-of-time is God's."*

Hurricanes and earthquakes come in cycles. A hurricane of massive proportions would fit perfectly the above prophetic phrases and statements.

Following is a summation of the scenario we are currently faced with. Astoundingly, it was penned more than 100 years ago.

> **"The East River will overflow and Brooklyn will be destroyed, and the Hudson River will overflow and New York will be destroyed; and then there will be a great earthquake and the two rivers will forsake their beds..."**
>
> (p. 61, *Trumpet Peals: A Collection of Timely and Eloquent Extracts from the Sermons of the Rev. T. De Witt Talmage, D.D.*, Broomfield & Company, New York, 1890).

The preacher who stated this was ahead of his time. What he proclaimed 120 years ago, is exactly what the seismologists and meteorologists see and predict as imminent today.

> **...meteorologists are saying that Long Island is at a very real risk of being the target of a natural disaster in the near future**...
>
> When it comes to the wrath of nature—in the form of hurricanes or other disasters—the odds are stacked against us. Many Long Islanders think of California as earthquake central for this country, not realizing that **New York City is**

riddled with active geological faults. But the probability of a major earthquake occurring in the Eastern United States before the year 2010 is nearly 100 percent, according to the Multidisciplinary Center for Earthquake Engineering Research. **Another sobering possibility is that a Katrina-magnitude storm will strike the New York metropolitan area. The likelihood that a major hurricane (Category 3 or higher) would hit New York City and Long Island in 2006 is one in 11,** according to Scott A. Mandia, professor of physical sciences at Suffolk County Community College.

(*Long Island Press*, "Blown Away: The Next Great Hurricane Will Hit L.I. Sooner Or Later," By April Jimenez 09/21/2006, *http://www.longislandpress.com*).

Meteorologists had targeted Long Island for a major hurricane in 2006. **Now that 2006 has passed, it does not mean we are in the clear. It only means we are living on borrowed time.**

"The worst possible thing that could happen is for us to have a minimal season this year [2006], because people were expecting an active season," said Professor Scott A. Mandia, of Suffolk County Community College, "It's like the boy who cried wolf! Now, next year [*and following*] people will be too relaxed, and that is very dangerous."

The cycles of time do not present us with exact dates to watch for. **Cycles give us approximations of the times we can expect re-occurrences** of natural and catastrophic events. Disasters of the past can sometimes warn us of future calamity. We need to pay attention.

The Island [Long Island] was hit with its own Katrina-type storm nearly 70 years ago, on Sept. 21, 1938. The Long Island Express, a Category 3 hurricane, devastated the East End and killed 600 people on Long Island and New England. Peak gusts hit LI at over 100 mph and peak storm surges were 12 feet above normal high tide. To place this in perspective, Hurricane Gloria, which paralyzed some of LI for up to 10 days in 1985, made landfall in LI as a Category 2, with winds reaching up to 85 mph and storm surges peaking at 6.9 feet. Simply put, **a Category 3 storm would totally ravage Long Island**. "If that [the 1938 hurricane] were to hit today in the same area, it would rival Hurricane Andrew (the Category 5 hurricane that hit Southern Florida and the Bahamas in 1992), if not more so, as far as damage done," Mike Wiley, the meteorologist in charge of the National Weather Service's forecasting office on Long Island, told the Wall Street Journal. If the most powerful winds hit closer to New York City, he added, "It would surpass the damage that we just saw with Hurricane Katrina." As he states it, "statistically, **we're overdue**."

(*Long Island Press*, "Blown Away: The Next Great Hurricane Will Hit L.I. Sooner Or Later," By April Jimenez 09/21/2006, *http://www.longislandpress.com*).

Long Island is due for a devastating hurricane like the one that hit on September 21, 1938:

That morning a *New York Times* editorial entitled "Hurricane" concluded, "*Every year an average of three such whirlwinds sweep the tropical North Atlantic between June and November. In 1933, there was an all-time record of twenty. If New York and the rest of the world have been so well informed about the cyclone, it is because of an admirable organized meteorological service*" (Allen, 1976). ... Later that day, **the greatest weather disaster ever to hit Long Island and New England** struck in the form of a category 3 hurricane. Long Island, New York and New England were changed forever by the *Long*

Island Express. The immediate effect of this powerful hurricane was to decimate many Long Island communities in terms of human and economic losses, however, the long term effects linger today. The '38 Hurricane ***created the Shinnecock Inlet*** and ***widened Moriches Inlet*** which, to this day, are changing the landscape of the south shore due to their influence on the natural littoral sand transport. History has shown that these powerful storms are rare but do in fact occur with long-term frequency. Case studies have shown that **the next time a storm like the Long Island Express roars through, it might be the greatest disaster in U.S. history.** (*http://www2.sunysuffolk.edu/mandias/38hurricane*).

A major obstacle to overcome is public complacency. Approximately 78.5% of current New York State coastal residents have never experienced a major hurricane (Hughes). One must remember that **in 1938, Long Island was mostly undeveloped.** The next time a major hurricane hits, it will be impacting a highly-urbanized region. ...there is a misguided sense that Long Island can withstand "strong" hurricanes with only minor inconveniences because few have ever experienced a major hurricane. ...the Long Island and New York City regions, would suffer greatly.

...the 1938 hurricane today would be considered the 6th costliest of all time. In 1998 dollars, the damage would be nearly $18 billion.

Experts now believe that **after Miami and New Orleans, New York City is considered the third most dangerous major city for the next hurricane disaster.** According to a 1990 study by the US Army Corps of Engineers, the city has some unique and **potentially lethal features. New York's major bridges such as the Verrazano Narrows and the George Washington are so high that they would experience hurricane force winds well before those winds were felt at sea-level locations. Therefore, these escape routes would have to be closed well before ground-level bridges (Time, 1998). The two ferry services across the Long Island Sound would also be shut down 6-12 hours before the storm surge invaded the waters around Long Island, further decreasing the potential for evacuation.**

A storm surge prediction program used by forecasters called *SLOSH* (Sea, Lake, and Overland Surge from Hurricanes) has predicted that in a category 4 hurricane, **John F. Kennedy International Airport would be under 20 feet of water and sea water would pour through the Holland and Brooklyn-Battery tunnels and into the city's subways throughout lower Manhattan.** The report did not estimate casualties, but did state that **storms "that would present low to moderate hazards in other regions of the country could result in heavy loss of life" in the New York City area** (Time, 1998).

...Surviving "Day One" of the hurricane is only part of the concern. Most people away from the coast believe that they are far enough inland to be safe from hurricanes. In one sense that is true for the immediate effects of the hurricane. **However, most of these inland residents fail to realize that their daily lives will be severely impacted for weeks or months.** Employees will not be able to get to work due to downed trees and widespread power outages may shut down the economy for quite a long time. According to the *LIPA Forecasts Hurricane Outages & Recovery,* Sept. 10,

2003, **a direct hit by a Category 3 hurricane could cause some 750,000 to 1,000,000 power outages island-wide.** And, it could take 15 to 30 days to restore service to all customers, or at least to those customers whose homes or businesses were not destroyed. (*http://www2.sunysuffolk.edu/mandias/38hurricane/hurricane_future.html*).

Hurricane storm surge causes approximately 90% of all storm deaths and injuries and much of the damage, therefore it is important for residents of Long Island, New York to be aware of the areas that will be affected by the storm surge. **The southern shore of Long Island is most vulnerable to storm surge inundation** because hurricane landfall will first occur there and **the low elevation will allow sea water to move well inland. ...*the storm surge height for a category 4 hurricane would be 29 feet above normal sea-level.*** (*http://www2.sunysuffolk.edu/mandias/38hurricane/storm_surge_maps.html*).

STORMS ARE GETTING STRONGER

In his film, An Inconvenient Truth, Al Gore states that Global Warming is producing hurricanes of greater magnitude than ever before. But people just do not heed the warnings.

"There have been warnings that hurricanes would get stronger. There were warnings that this hurricane [Katrina]—days before it hit—would breach the levees, would cause the kind of damage that it ultimately did cause. And one question, we as a people, need to decide, is how we react when we hear warnings from the leading scientists in the world." (*An Inconvenient Truth*).

SUPER STORM

Science predicts greater hurricanes, so does the Bible. Both the code and the literal surface text of Ezekiel 7 refer to the judgment of God. If it comes in the form of a hurricane it will probably be the most destructive super-storm in modern history. The physical aspects described in the prophecies coincide with scientific evidence. The horrifying scenarios presented by the meteorological service will be exemplified by the raging furry that Yahweh unleashes when he decides it is time to execute judgment.

DEADLY QUAKE

Geologically speaking, New York is building up for a major earthquake. Could it be one of the great earthquakes of the Apocalypse spoken of in the book of Revelation?

> And the same hour was there a great earthquake, and the **tenth part of the city fell**, and in the earthquake were **slain of men seven thousand**: and the remnant were affrighted, and gave glory to the God of heaven.
> The **second woe** is past; and, behold, the **third woe** cometh quickly.
> And the seventh angel sounded; and there were great voices in heaven, saying, The kingdoms of this world are become the kingdoms of our Lord, and of his Christ; and he shall reign for ever and ever.

(Revelation 11:13-15).

Interestingly, these Revelation verses state, *the second woe is past*, and the Ezekiel New York grid has two woes symmetrically crossed. If one tenth of the city falls and 7,000 men die it seems mild considering the size and population of the city.

Many scholars agree that the book of Revelation was found in parts and fragments, not as a whole assembled manuscript. It was pieced together and perhaps not in proper order. The verses just quoted from Revelation chapter eleven seem to be speaking of the coming of Christ. The following passages from Revelation sixteen also appear to refer to the coming of Christ, and portray a much more severe picture. It defines an earthquake like never before experienced.

Behold, I come as a thief. Blessed is he that watcheth, and keepeth his garments, lest he walk naked, and they see his shame.

And he gathered them together into a place called in the Hebrew tongue **Armageddon**. *

[*n. *Armageddon: "Mount of the Congregation." New York Metropolis is the largest US congregation of Jewish people. The largest number are in Brooklyn. The only city in the world with more Jews is Tel Aviv, Israel.*]

And the seventh angel poured out his vial into the air; and there came a great voice out of the temple of heaven, from the throne, saying, It is done.

And there were voices, and thunders, and lightnings; and there was a **great earthquake, such as was not since men were upon the earth**, so mighty an earthquake, and so great.

And **the great city was divided into three parts**, and the cities of the nations fell: and great Babylon came in remembrance before God, to give unto her the cup of the wine of the fierceness of his wrath.

And **every island fled away**, and the mountains were not found.

And there fell upon men a great hail out of heaven, every stone about the weight of a talent: and men blasphemed God because of the plague of the hail; for the plague thereof was exceeding great.

(Revelation 16:15-21).

"**Every island fled away**." New York City has **thirty islands**, all of which may suffer devastation: *Barren Island, The Blauzes, Broad Channel Island, Chimney Sweeps, City Island, Coney Island, Ellis Island, Governors Island, Hart Island, High Island, Hoffman Island, Hunters Island, Isle of Meadow, Liberty Island, Long Island, Manhattan, Mill Rock, North Brother Island, Prall's Island, Randall's Island, Rat Island, Rikers Island, Roosevelt Island, Shooters Island, South Brother Island, Staten Island, Swinburne Island, Twin Island, U Thant Island, Ward's Island* (http://en.wikipedia.org/).

"And the mountains were not found." Many scholars believe that the references to **mountains** in this passage could pertain to the sky scraper **buildings** in the city. If massive earthquakes level the buildings in the city, the symbolic "mountains" will no longer be found.

SEISMIC TIME BOMB

Chimneys and balconies fall off buildings, blocking streets to traffic. Failed signals trap thousands of people underground in subways. Fires break out from damaged electrical wires.

That could well be the scenario should a big earthquake jolt New York City.

The possibility exists that a considerable quake will rattle the nation's most populous city within the next few decades, seismologists say. The metropolis lies on several faults, along which tremors tend to occur. While most New Yorkers are probably blissfully unaware of the potential hazard, city planners are preparing for the worst, but experts warn that they may not be doing enough.

(*Waiting for the big one: Is New York prepared for earthquakes?* By Zakir Hussain, *http://jscms.jrn.columbia.edu/cns/2005-02-15/hussain-earthquake*).

Chuck Scarborough, news anchor: We are sitting on a seismic time bomb.

...WNBC-TV anchor Chuck Scarborough is known for his calm, cool demeanor. But when it comes to a major earthquake in the New York area, he has been sounding the alarm for nearly 20 years:

Scarborough: It's going to happen some day. The question is are we going to be ready? And we aren't now. The structures here simply are not built strongly enough to withstand a quake and it would be a major disaster. ...

Scarborough: The fact is that we are in an area that does have seismic activity, that has a billion year history of seismic activity, that has significant earthquakes from time to time. They don't happen nearly as often as they do in the West Coast. But there are reputable seismologists who'll tell you that **we're overdue right now.** ...

Mary Lou Zoback, U.S.G.S.: There are a number of faults that we recognize running beneath New York. There are moderate to small earthquakes. And that always indicates there is potential for larger earthquakes. ...

(*Are You Prepared for the Next Big One? U.S. scientists say it's not a question of if, but when*, 2006, By Hoda Kotb, Correspondent NBC News; *http://standeyo.com/ NEWS/06_Earth_Changes/060608.ready.4Big.1.html*).

...many scientists agree: A quake is coming. And New York isn't ready for it. ...no one denies we're going to see an earthquake in New York City. ...

Columbia University seismologist Klaus Jacob knows why. **It's those two damn 5's. Historically, two significant earthquakes have rattled New York—one in 1737, another in 1884. Both measured around magnitude (M) 5.0 on the Richter scale. Since both emanated from roughly the same spot in Rockaway, 147 years apart,**

and it's been 111 years since the last one
[stated on December 11, 1995, thus now, in 2006,
122 years since the last one]**, you'd have to say
there's a pretty decent likelihood of
another M5 coming out of Rockaway
within the next 50 years** [probably less than 25
years].

… the idea of an M5 just doesn't scare anyone. …
just because our short-term memory includes only
two 5's doesn't mean we're limited to them in the
future. **We could easily have a 6, a 7** [or
greater].

At what point, Jacob wonders, do people start
listening? "So what is the critical earthquake
around here?" he says. "Five-point-eight. And **as
you approach a 6, it gets dangerous. Now,
if you go beyond 6"**—his voice drops to a
stage whisper—**"nobody knows what's
gonna happen.** A magnitude 6 would probably
have the potential to come close to what the 7 did
in Kobe. And **if we ever would have a 7 in
this area—forget it! I mean, there will be
no Metropolitan Museum, no Museum of
Modern Art, no Lincoln Center. Forget it.
New York as we know it as a cultural,
business, population institution will not
exist if we have a 7."**

Alan Kafka, a geophysicist at Boston College's
Weston Observatory, will take Jacob even a step
further. Kafka says **it would be only
"scientifically conservative" to wonder
why New York City couldn't have an M8
quake.**

("New York Earthquake: The Quake Next Time—Waiting
for the Big One," by Fred Graver and Charlie Rubin,
December 11, 1995, *Compuserve New York Magazine Online,
http://www.geo.sunysb.edu/classes/oldclasses/GEO201/NYearthqu
ake.htm*).

MAJOR FAULT DISSECTS NEW YORK

The Metropolitan area of New York centers directly on a major fault line that runs right up the East River between Manhattan and Long Island.

...About 400 million years ago, Africa collided with North America, swallowing a proto-Atlantic ocean called the Iapetus Ocean, in what geologists call "subduction." In closing, it left behind a **suturelike geological formation known as Cameron's Line, which [stretches from central Massachusetts] runs through the Bronx, down the East River, past Gracie Mansion, under the Queensboro Bridge, through Staten Island, and all the way down to Charleston, South Carolina** [over 900 miles].

The red sandstone and brownstone you find in the Palisades is the same as you'll see in the rift valleys of Central Africa. We have similar east-west rifts in our rock. And **these rifts share another trait: a tendency to produce earthquakes of magnitude 7 or 7.5.**

...Klaus Jacob warns, **"We have so many faults here in New York from a long geological history that it doesn't matter. It can be any and all of those faults that can go. So we have to decide that the earthquake could occur anywhere."**

(*ibid.*).

RECENT NEW YORK QUAKES

Two mild earthquakes struck New York City in January and October of 2001. This may be a wake-up call telling us the Earth is about to become violent.

17 January 2001, At 7:34 AM EST a magnitude 2.4 tremor struck the upper east side of Manhattan (40.777°N latitude and 73.954°W longitude). The epicenter of the quake plots near the vicinity of 102nd Street and Park Avenue …

The truly fascinating aspect of the quake was that the epicenter was located on the mapped trace of the 125th Street **(Manhattanville) fault** that **traverses diagonally** across Manhattan from Broadway and 125th Street **southeastward** to the Harlem Meer in Central Park (108th Street), passing through the epicenter across to 96th Street and the east shore of Manhattan. From there the **Manhattanville fault** passes across the East River and onwards to the subsurface of **Long Island City.**

The event, marking the **first recorded historic earthquake to strike on land within the confines of the NYC metropolitan area**, was felt throughout the city. Larger previous earthquakes in the vicinity of NYC were recorded in 1884 (M-5.0-5.5), 1783 (M-4.9), and 1737 (M-5.2).

…a Dukelabs geologist has mapped **many NW-trending faults** in the Queens Tunnel (Merguerian 2002b) …the **NW-trending faults** in NYC …hold the greatest potential for urban seismic risk.

27 October 2001, At 5:42 AM EST a magnitude 2.6 tremor struck the west side of Manhattan (40.76°N latitude and 73.98°W longitude). … These events are significant because they mark **the first recorded on-land earthquakes to occur within the confines of New York City.**

(*SMALL EARTHQUAKES STRIKE NYC, http://www.dukelabs.com/NYC%20Quake/NYCQuake.htm*).

These two New York City earthquakes in 2001, should really get our attention, that there is pressure built-up in the strata beneath the metropolis. Rock layers trying to push in opposite directions create enormous tension that eventually releases in the form of earthquakes when the jagged rocks finally slip. Since these two quakes were small they could not relieve much of the stored pressure. The tensile energy that has accumulated may be getting ready to tear the city apart.

SPLITTING LONG ISLAND

The first of these recent quakes occurred on the **Manhattanville fault** that comes from the northwest of Manhattan, crosses the East River and goes directly through **Long Island City**.

Charles Merguerian, chairman of Hofstra University's geology department, prepared a fault map that shows the Manhattanville fault crossing Manhattan and going through Long Island City, and passing right through the campus of LaGuardia Community College.

LaGuardia Community College of the City University of New York [**CUNY**] is named for Fiorello H. LaGuardia, New York City's New Deal mayor, who united and inspired a city of immigrants. Located at a transit hub that links Queens, the most ethnically diverse borough, with the world center of finance, commerce and the arts ... (*http://portal.cuny.edu*).

The **City University of New York** (**CUNY; acronym usually pronounced "kyoo-nee" or "coo-nee"**), located in New York City, is the largest urban university in the United States, with more than 208,000 enrolled in degree programs and another 208,000 enrolled in adult and continuing education courses at campuses in all five boroughs. (*http://en.wikipedia.org/wiki/CUNY*).

The Ezekiel 7, New York Bible Code, says Long Island will be crushed, pounded, divided, cut, and now we see that **one of the fault lines that has demonstrated movement passes right through Long Island City**. Not only that, but it cuts right through under the the campus of **La Guardia Community College**, part of the **CUNY** system.

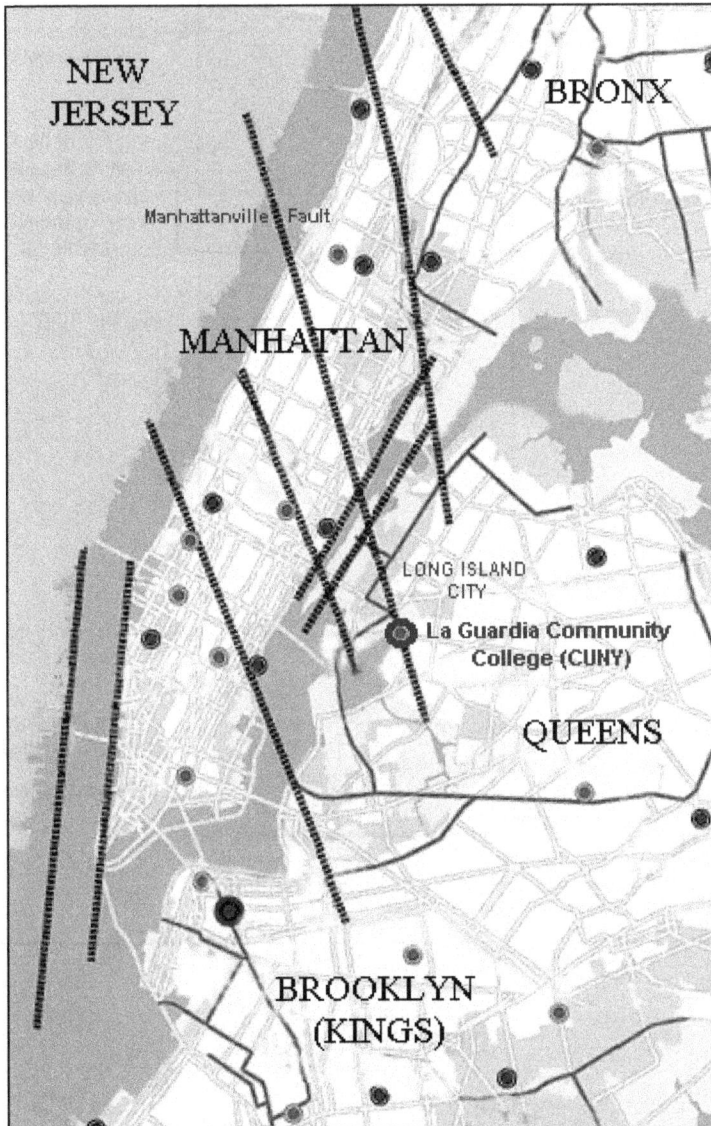

NYC Faults according to Professor Charles Merguerian data

New York
Ezekiel 6:13 through 7:8 Matrix 15 Skip

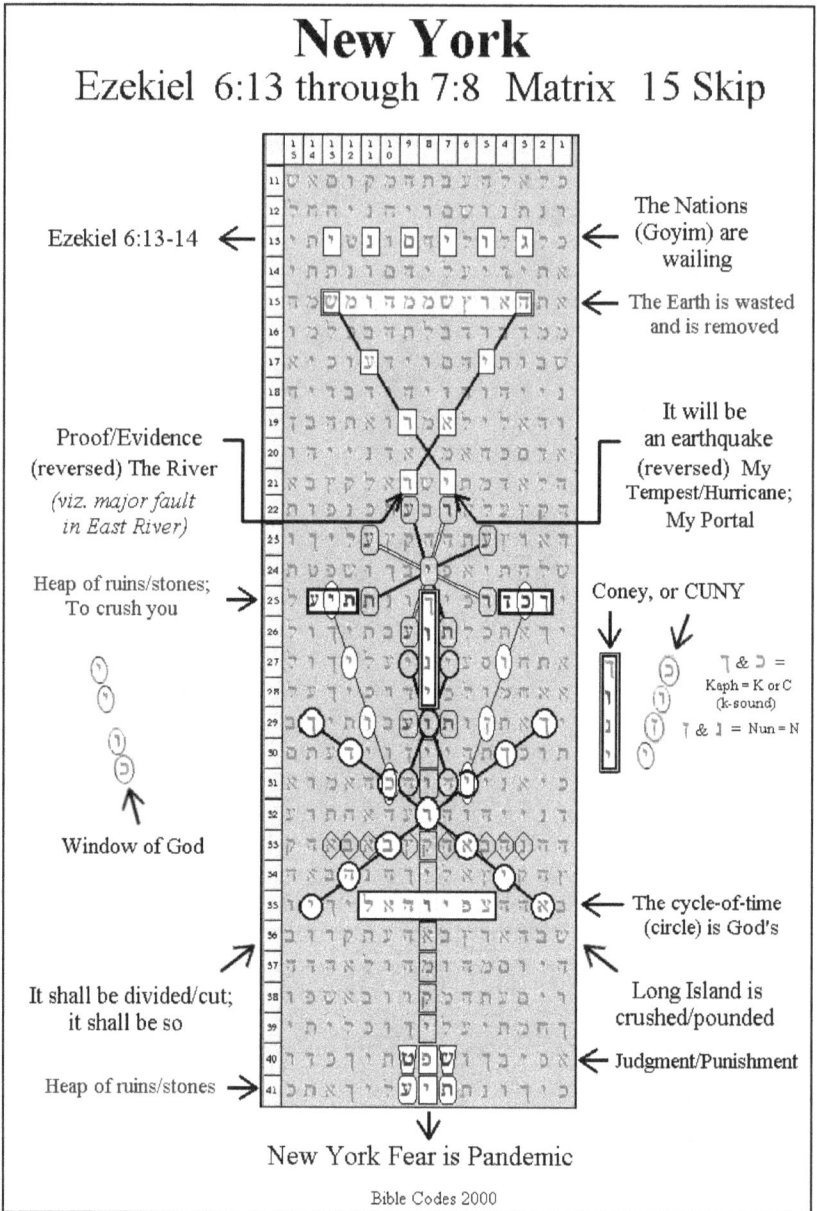

Ezekiel 6:13-14 ←

The Nations
(Goyim) are
wailing

The Earth is wasted
and is removed

It will be
an earthquake
(reversed) My
Tempest/Hurricane;
My Portal

Proof/Evidence
(reversed) The River
*(viz. major fault
in East River)*

Heap of ruins/stones;
To crush you

Window of God

Coney, or CUNY

ך & כ =
Kaph = K or C
(k-sound)

ן & נ = Nun = N

The cycle-of-time
(circle) is God's

It shall be divided/cut;
it shall be so

Long Island is
crushed/pounded

Heap of ruins/stones →

Judgment/Punishment

New York Fear is Pandemic

Bible Codes 2000

CONEY OR CUNY

Coney is spelled כוני. In this grid it appears as כוין and ךוני. This is due to the use of the *sof* letters which are treated the same as initial letters in the codes.

The Hebrew characters that spell CUNY, כוני, are the same letters that spell Coney (the second letter, Waw, can be a W, U, or O). In unpointed script these two words appear identical. The references to Coney (Island) in the code, might serve a dual purpose and also pertain to CUNY (college campus), especially since we see the Long Island split/fault right beneath the LaGuardia CUNY Campus.

LIQUID EARTH

...a New York 5 could easily pack the wallop of a California 6. Even building commissioner Joel Miele admits, carefully, that "the moderate earthquake could be, locally, more than moderate." Moreover, a larger overall geographic area is at risk here, because **earthquake shaking transmits much more efficiently in the East than in the West.**

...Seismologist[s] described the ground in Flushing as "Jell-O." Said one, **"If you're looking for a poor location, from a seismic perspective, you would not want to live in Flushing." Or, he quickly added, the eastern part of the Bronx. Or off Rockaway. Rockaway: home of the 5.** In Rockaway, in Howard Beach, out to the peninsula, you dig down two feet and you find water. **The word that keeps coming up for the Rockaways is liquefaction.** Imagine you're standing at the edge of a beach, wiggling your feet on dry sand and suddenly you're sinking into the water.

That's liquefaction. That's the soil in Rockaway. **Liquefaction is the abrupt transformation of soil into fluid by repeated earthquake vibrations**—the sands lose their friction resistance and just give way.

("New York Earthquake: The Quake Next Time—Waiting

for the Big One," by Fred Graver and Charlie Rubin, December 11, 1995, *Compuserve New York Magazine Online*, *http://www.geo.sunysb.edu/classes/oldclasses/GEO201/NYearthqu ake.htm*).

If nature happens to align itself and the earth shakes violently out of control, at the same time the wind and the waves rise to occasion, New York City could be battered into oblivion.

A quake of any size would have the potential to destroy bridges and tunnels completely severing Long Island from Manhattan, the Bronx, and the mainland.

Flushing and Rockaway are prone to liquefaction. With Flushing on the north and Rockaway on the south, if the faults between them started shaking it could split the island. Even the solid land turns to mush with enough shaking. The earth becomes fluid, as if it were liquid. A simultaneous hurricane, even of modest size, could wash all that mush out to sea, like so much sediment floating in a River current.

A north to south rift could slice through Queens dividing the island. Another quake following along the Manhattanville Fault Line could cut right through Long Island City further dividing the island by creating a north-west to south-east rift splitting apart Queens and Kings right down the line.

Queens would be in two sections. One side would be across a moat from Brooklyn. The rest of Queens and Long Island would be severed completely away, standing further to the east. **The great city would be divided into three** (see, Speculative map of NYC and Long Island, quake/storm aftermath, p.82).

The Cameron's Line fault has the known prehistoric potential to swallow up massive amounts of the Earth's surface. A major earthquake on Cameron's Line could completely swallow Manhattan, Staten Island, and much more.

> ...the Manhattan waterfront was built up with hydraulic fill, material dredged by barge or pumped and dumped there to reclaim land from the sea and enlarge the harbor facilities. Today, **that soil would be sandy and loose, below**

the water table, and a prime candidate for liquefaction.

"...around the Brooklyn Battery Tunnel, that whole area is reclaimed from the bay, from the 1800s on. When they tried to put in a sewer using a vibratory pile driver, they collapsed four two-family homes within two blocks. Killed a woman. Imagine what an earthquake can do." ...

When a quake hits a city, it doesn't hit the entire city in the same way. Quakes move in waves, both up and down and back and forth. They disperse at different amplitudes and frequencies. Distance from the epicenter of the quake is another determining factor in how you'll feel its force, and all these ground motions and rampaging split signals get aided by soil conditions. (*ibid.*).

TSUNAMI

Besides the liquefaction caused by the earthquake frequencies, there is the possibility of simultaneous hurricane action and even the chance of a tsunami, that would certainly flush away any remaining *liquid-earth* created by the relentless shaking from beneath.

...the quake that generated the recent Asian tsunami measured 9.0 ...

An earthquake along the East Coast could wreak damage over a greater area than one of similar magnitude along the West Coast, says David Russ of the U.S. Geological Service in Reston, Va. Because the earth's crust is colder and more brittle on the East Coast, seismic energy transmits more efficiently.

...John Mutter of Columbia's Earth Institute said

a tsunami could occur here. "To say it could not happen is not true," he told a gathering in Manhattan ...

(Waiting for the big one: Is New York prepared for earthquakes? By Zakir Hussain, http://jscms.jrn.columbia.edu/cns/2005-02-15/hussain-earthquake).

LIQUEFACTION IN THE BIBLE

Scripture talks about the land melting, "And the Lord Yahweh of hosts is he that toucheth the land, and it shall melt, and all that dwell therein shall mourn: and it [*the land*] shall rise up wholly like a flood..." (Amos 9:5, cf. 8:8). "The mountains quake at him, and the hills melt, and the earth is burned at his presence, yea, the world, and all that dwell therein." (Nahum 1:5). That is basically what will happen when we experience liquefaction. The earth will quake, and the shaking will literally dissolve the land and cause it to become like water, like a flood. The earth will move in waves. Structures will sink like in quicksand. If all hell breaks loose at once like the Bible predicts, it will be a scene none of us will want to see, and few who see it will survive.

EARTHQUAKE STORM

An "earthquake storm," is a **sequence of large earthquakes that sweep across a large area**, according to *The Exodus Decoded* (History Channel).

If all the faults in Manhattan shake lose at once it could literally break the island into a thousand little pieces, and the Cameron Line fault could be the catalyst to set the earth shaking, and could also be the rift to swallow all the debris. Manhattan and the Bronx would be gone forever. Staten Island could fall into that same trench. The only remains would be the remnants of Brooklyn and Long Island, and they would be totally ravaged.

HELP IS SUNK

Those who may survive the initial destruction and havoc will have a hard time finding medical help, since most of the hospitals will have sunk into the earth. Most of these Trauma Centers, equipped to handle large numbers of disaster victims are situated along or near the fault lines in areas prone to liquefaction. Any or all of these faults could be quaking.

...A number of key hospitals—Bellevue, Albert Einstein, Beth Israel, and St. Vincent's—sit on soil with a greater than 50 percent probability of liquefaction....

("New York Earthquake: The Quake Next Time—Waiting for the Big One," by Fred Graver and Charlie Rubin, December 11, 1995, *Compuserve New York Magazine Online, http://www.geo.sunysb.edu/classes/oldclasses/GEO201/NYearthqu ake.htm*).

Most of the Evacuation Reception Centers, for hurricane evacuees are also in the areas of faults and liquefaction. If hurricanes and earthquakes hit simultaneously there will be no place to go. There will certainly be no way out of the metropolis.

Without bridges and airports—Kennedy and LaGuardia are sitting on "Jell-O" (*ibid.*)—victims cannot escape, and help cannot get in. Whatever is left of the city streets, nothing will be moving. Abandoned cars will be blocking the streets and sidewalks.

BLAZING INFERNO

Besides all the direct damage from the earthquake's shaking and sinking, there will most certainly be broken gas pipes belching flames all around, causing additional danger as secondary blazes erupt everywhere. Anything within reach of the flames will ignite and fires will be blazing out of control. The entire remains of the city could potentially become a raging inferno. A study "estimated that a quake would cause more than 130 simultaneous blazes." (*Cities at Risk for Earthquakes: New York City,*

Fire is always the devil child of an earthquake —what if a twenty-story building was burning and firemen couldn't get their water up higher than a few stories? "An earthquake produces a tinderbox of exposed wood, flying dust, and broken gas lines," says Charles Scawthorn. "The potential for fire increases with every degree of magnitude. As does the potential for breakage in the water system. **The big question is whether we'll have the water supply to fight these fires, and to sustain life** in the city."

"They are in complete denial!" shouts Klaus Jacob. "They have essentially **two supply lines** bringing water to New York, and **one is leaking already. It happens to be close to a fault** where there was once an earthquake ..." (*ibid.*).

Large-scale disasters such as fires, hurricanes or earthquakes are rare in New York City. But given the area's 8.1 million inhabitants, dense construction and commercial importance, the ramifications of even a moderate earthquake or hurricane would be catastrophic nationwide.

...the ultra rich and the most impoverished would be equally in harm's way. But one characteristic links all of the places here most in danger: high population density.

...the New York metropolitan area encompasses some 21 million residents, one-seventh of the entire U.S. population.

...a disaster to this region would touch nearly every corner of the country. *That New York City lies atop a messy crisscross of fault lines and sits at a precarious angle of Atlantic and Arctic winds, then, is of national importance.*

(*In Event of Natural Disaster, City's 8 Million Residents Would Be In Trouble, Experts Say*, by Michal Lumsden, *http://www.columbiajournalist.org/rw1_muha/2005/article.asp?subj=city &course=rw1_muha&id=663*).

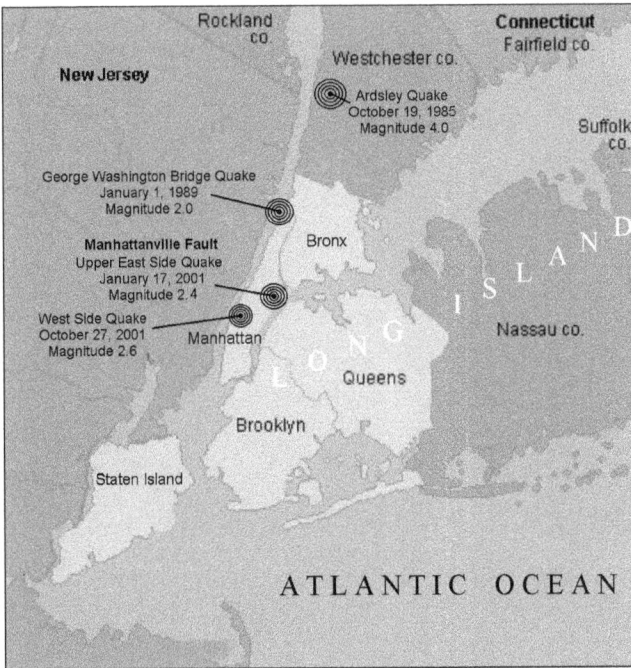

Locations of recent earthquakes in New York

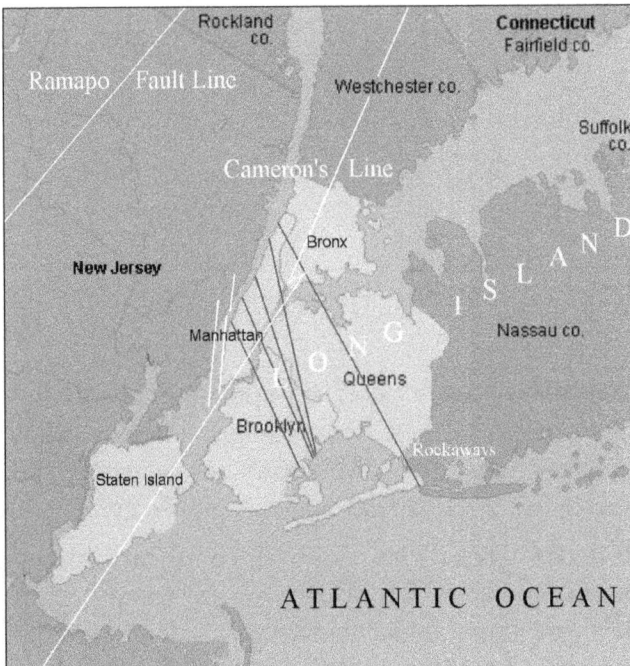

NYC fault map, referenced from Merguerian data.

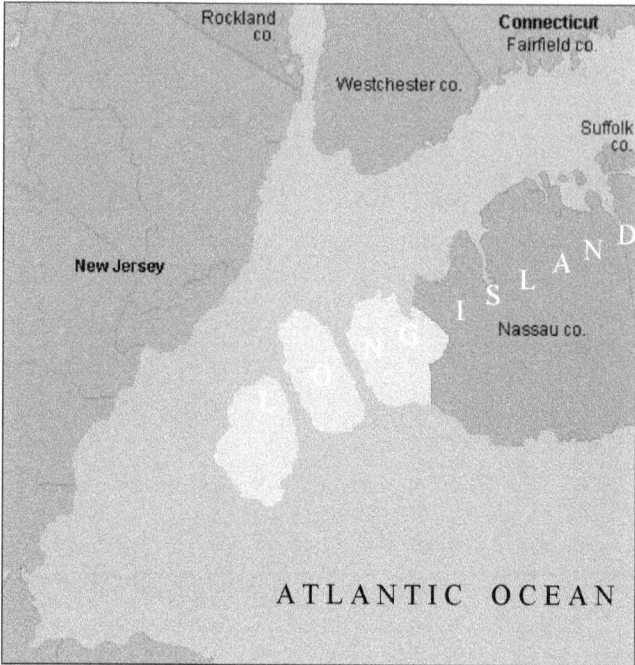

Speculative map of NYC and Long Island, quake/storm aftermath.
Remainder of the metropolis divided into three parts. (Worst-case scenario?)

We may be calculating a worst-case scenario, but on the other hand, according to Biblical prophecy it may even be far worse than we would ever dare to imagine.

DIVIDED INTO THREE

And there were voices, and thunders, and lightnings; and there was a **great earthquake, such as was not since men were upon the earth**, so mighty an earthquake, and so great.

And **the great city was divided into three parts**, and the cities of the nations fell: and great Babylon came in remembrance before God, to give unto her the cup of the wine of the fierceness of his wrath. (Revelation 16:18-19).

THE REASONS WE ARE WARNED

Isaiah, chapter 48

1: Hear ye this, O house of Jacob, which are called by the name of Israel, and are come forth out of the waters of Judah, which swear by the name of Yahweh, and make mention of the God of Israel, but not in truth, nor in righteousness.

2: For they call themselves of the holy city, and stay themselves upon the God of Israel; Yahweh of hosts is his name.

3: I have declared the former things from the beginning; and they went forth out of my mouth, and I shewed them; I did them suddenly, and they came to pass.

4: Because I knew that thou art obstinate, and thy neck is an iron sinew, and thy brow brass;

5: I have even from the beginning declared it to thee; before it came to pass I shewed it thee: lest thou shouldest say, Mine idol hath done them, and my graven image, and my molten image, hath commanded them.

6: Thou hast heard, see all this; and will not ye declare it? I have shewed thee new things from this time, even hidden things, and thou didst not know them.

7: They are created now, and not from the beginning; even before the day when thou heardest them not; lest thou shouldest say, Behold, I knew them.

8: Yea, thou heardest not; yea, thou knewest not; yea, from that time that thine ear was not opened: for I knew that thou wouldest deal very treacherously, and wast called a transgressor from the womb.

9: **For my name's sake** will I defer mine anger, and for my praise will I refrain for thee, that I cut thee not off.

10: Behold, I have refined thee, but not with silver; I have chosen thee in the furnace of affliction.

11: For mine own sake, even for mine own sake, will I do it: for **how should my name be polluted?** and I will not give my glory unto another.

12: Hearken unto me, O Jacob and **Israel, my called**; I am he; I am the first, I also am the last.

13: Mine hand also hath laid the foundation of the earth, and my right hand hath spanned the heavens: when I call unto them, they stand up together.

14: All ye, assemble yourselves, and hear; which among them hath declared these things? Yahweh hath loved him: he will do his pleasure on Babylon, and his arm shall be on the Chaldeans.

15: I, even I, have spoken; yea, I have called him: I have brought him, and he shall make his way prosperous.

16: Come ye near unto me, hear ye this; I have not spoken in secret **from the beginning; from the time that it was, there am I: and now the Lord Yahweh, and his Spirit, hath sent me.**

17: **Thus saith Yahweh, thy Redeemer, the Holy One of Israel**; I am Yahweh thy God which teacheth thee to profit, which leadeth thee by the way that thou shouldest go.

18: O that thou hadst hearkened to my commandments! then had thy peace been as a river, and thy righteousness as the waves of the sea:

19: Thy seed also had been as the sand, and the offspring of thy bowels like the gravel thereof; **his** *name should not have been cut off* nor destroyed from before me.

20: Go ye forth of Babylon, flee ye from the Chaldeans, with a voice of singing declare ye, tell this, utter it even to the end of the earth; say ye, **Yahweh hath redeemed his servant Jacob [Israel]**.

21: And they thirsted not when he led them through the deserts: he caused the waters to flow out of the rock for them: he clave the rock also, and the waters gushed out.

22: **There is no peace, saith Yahweh, unto the wicked.**

COME OUT OF HER

The United States is Israel, via Manasseh, but the U.S. is also the end-time Babylon. Thus it is evident that in some sense Israel is in bondage within Babylon. Just as there was a dual Babylon in ancient times, the Kingdom of Babylon and the city of Babylon, our modern Babylon also has a dual title: New York, New York.

By employing the A=6 alpha-numeric system, B=12, C=18, D=27... Z=156, and then adding each of the numerical values of the letters in New York, the total is 666. *New York, New York*, is a double confirmation of the number 666, that is the identifying number of the Beast and the beast-system.

When Yahweh warns to flee out of Babylon is he warning to get out of New York? Is he talking to you?

Revelation 18

[2] And he cried mightily with a strong voice, saying, Babylon the great is fallen, is fallen, and is become the habitation of devils, and the hold of

every foul spirit, and a cage of every unclean and hateful bird.

[**3**] For all nations have drunk of the wine of the wrath of her fornication, and the kings of the earth have committed fornication with her, and the merchants of the earth are waxed rich through the abundance of her delicacies.

[**4**] And I heard another voice from heaven, saying, **Come out of her, my people, that ye be not partakers of her sins, and that ye receive not of her plagues.**

[**5**] For her sins have reached unto heaven, and God hath remembered her iniquities.

[**6**] Reward her even as she rewarded you, and **double unto her double** according to her works: in the cup which she hath filled fill to her double.

[**7**] How much she hath glorified herself, and lived deliciously, so much torment and sorrow give her: for she saith in her heart, I sit a queen, and am no widow, and shall see no sorrow.

[**8**] Therefore shall her plagues come in one day, death, and mourning, and famine; and she shall be utterly burned with fire: for strong is the Yahweh God who judgeth her.

WARNING FROM BEYOND

Yahweh-God has sent us a message from beyond eternity. He saw the end from the beginning and wrote the Word before it happened. His Word is his attempt, through his prophets and scribes, to send his instructions to his people.

HIS SERVANT JACOB: END-TIME ISRAEL

Brit-Am ...identifies the USA with Manasseh and Britain and her daughters with Ephraim though we admit to an overlap in population and sometimes in aspects of identity. At all events with these general identifications in mind consider the following:

Feminine aspect more significant in Manasseh. Manasseh a nation of immigrants who forget troubles of the "Old Country" through newly found prosperity. Ephraim completes processes begun by Manasseh.

Manasseh to contain a good portion of Simeon [i.e. Welsh and Irish according to Brit-Am] both in the physical sense and in the sense of Tribal attributes. ***Manasseh the Tribe MOST dedicated to settling the Land of Israel***. Manasseh first deliberately forgets Moses and the Law he represents but later has the quality of returning to "Moses" due to an inner drive within the essence of Manasseh.

The name Manasseh [MNSH] in Hebrew is spelled the same as Moses [MSH] but with an extra letter "N" in Manasseh representing the quality of forgetting. Nevertheless Moses is still within Manasseh.

This quality is especially brought out through the ***attachment of Manasseh to the Land of Israel***. Manasseh to become great after Ephraim. Meshiach ben Yoseph (Messiah son of Joseph) to come from Manasseh. Manasseh to be involved with ***building of Third Temple***. Kings of Israel from Manasseh were more like "Princes" or "Presidents" when compared with the monarchs from Ephraim. ***The renewal of Israel will begin in the territory of Manasseh*** [i.e. U.S.A.].

(*Brit-Am Now*, #759)

WE ARE THE TEMPLE

The temple of Yahweh is renewed and rebuilt in us. There is no need for a rebuilding of the literal, physical, material temple. We have been shown clearly that we are the temple. God says he will not dwell in temples we build. That is a thing of the past. He is doing a new thing. He wants to dwell in us, to lead and guide us. That is his new covenant.

> **"Behold, I will send my messenger and he shall prepare the way before me: and Yahweh whom ye seek, shall suddenly come into his temple, even the messenger of the covenant, whom ye delight in..."** (Malachi 3:1). [*viz. i.e.* Your body is the temple].

The spiritual fulfillment of this prophetic verse happens when God fills you with his Holy Spirit, the Comforter. Yahweh is Yesu, the Comforter and the Holy Spirit, the messenger of the covenant. Yesu said, "[The Spirit of truth] dwelleth with you, and shall be in you. I will not leave you comfortless: I will come to you." (John 14:17-18).

PROMISED LAND

Will we ever return physically to the Land of Israel, or is the United States the promised land, as the early American Jews believed? In 1948 when the State of Israel was created, many Jews from around the world left their homes and moved to Israel. But most of the Jews in the U.S. Stayed here. They said this is the land of promise; why would we leave?

Many Jews do not see Zionists as true Jews but atheistic terrorists falsely reclaiming the Holy Land. Jews of the true lineage are persecuted by the Zionists.

...thousands of Jews gathered opposite the Israeli consulate in New York City to protests against the existence of the state of Israel and its ongoing persecution of religious Jews, Tuesday July 24, 2007. (*http://www.nkusa.org*).

Anti-Zionist Orthodox Jews protest Zionist occupation of the Holy Land and the creation of the Zionist state of "Israel". ...The founding of the State of "Israel" is in direct contradiction to the teachings of the Torah which forbids the establishment of a Jewish state and commands Jews to remain in exile until released from that exile by the Almighty Himself, without any human intervention, at which time all nations of the world will live together in peace and harmony. ...In this tragic time we pray for a speedy, peaceful, and painless dismantlement of the heretical Zionist state of "Israel".
(*http://www.nkusa.org/activities/Demonstrations/2007 0610.cfm*).

The U.S. Jewish population is greater than Israel's. There are 6,155,000 Jews in the United States, while Israel has only 5,025,000. The total world-wide number is 14,596,217.

The State of New York is the home of 1,657,000 Jews. "Both the highest number and highest percentage of Jews in the country..." *http://www.infoplease.com/askeds/us-jewish-population.html*).

An amazing **1,355,900** of this number **reside in the combined area of Long Island and the New York City Metropolitan area, including Staten Island**.

TWENTY-ONE MILLION LIVES ENDANGERED

Almost one million Jews are on Long Island alone. There may be more than double that many of the Lost House of Israel who do not even know they are Israelites. Brooklyn and Queens, the location where Long Island may soon be divided and cut through, are housing the outstanding number of 617,000 Jews. Manhattan has about one half that number. In contrast, Jerusalem has only 570,000.

The total population of all nationalities on Long Island including Brooklyn and Queens is 7,439,239. When the entire New York City is included along with Long Island the total population reaches over ten million. If the whole New York metropolitan area is devastated by earthquakes and hurricanes it will include the adjacent section of New Jersey, which brings the number to **over 21 million lives endangered**.

Approximately 1.5 million of this population are Jews. Add the probable number of "lost" Israel, perhaps double, reaching a total number of Judah and Israel at about 4.5 million. That is roughly a fourth of the total inhabitants of the designated area.

We are only talking here of the local population of metropolitan New York, that great city, and not of the total possible world-wide decimation if the disaster extends beyond New York.

THE CALLING

According to Scripture Yahweh is calling out his people. He wants to once again join together the houses of Judah and Israel to make one people and one nation, and he wants them to **come out of the idolatrous city** and not be destroyed with her.

The heart of this country is about to receive a great blow from which it will never recover. No matter where we are we will feel it. Nothing will ever be the same again.

You now have the facts and must decide what the implications are. Is the call to "Come out of her" referring to New York, or the entire U.S.? Is God speaking to you?

The U.S. Is both Babylon and Israel, and in a sense, Israel in the captivity of Babylon. Yahweh is calling Jews and Israelites (who do not yet know their identity) to come out of the great city. Non-Jewish Americans may or may not be Israelites through the birthright of Joseph. Whether you believe you are a Jew or a Gentile, this call is to everyone who has ears to hear. Regardless your identity, if you feel compelled to flee out of New York, then do so. You may save your life. No one knows exactly when New York will shake down, nor how severe it will actually be. But it does not look good.

When it all shakes loose if you are in the city your chances of survival are very slim.

God is beckoning the Jews and the lost tribes of the House of Israel (predominantly Christians) and anyone else who would escape.

What if you do not believe in God? Then ignore what the Bible and the Code have recorded. **Just look at the warnings the scientists of seismology and meteorology have issued**. Then decide if you should heed their words or not.

This is not a religious issue. This is a physical salvation, not spiritual. It is only a temporal solution. Anybody desiring spiritual deliverance and redemption must go a step further. Seek and ye shall find.

If you wake up tomorrow and Earth is still here, thank God you have another opportunity to consider, and to hope and pray you make the right decisions.

If you start planning your departure now, you may have time to escape before the city falls. You can do some research for a new location. You might even have a chance to prearrange for living accommodations and employment before leaving. But the longer you wait the less chance there is of this.

If you choose to leave the city, where do you go? Scripture suggests you flee into the mountains. "But **they that escape of them shall escape, and shall be on the**

mountains like doves of the valleys, all of them mourning, every one for his iniquity." (Ezekiel 7:16).

You can head west about 20 miles to the first set of mountains, but whether that is far enough is your guess. You will be right on the Ramapo Fault Line. It might be wise to go further just in case the earth quakes there too, when New York falls.

> So thou, O son of man, I have set thee a watchman *unto the house of Israel*; therefore **thou shalt hear the word at my mouth, and warn them from me**. (Ezekiel 33:7)
>
> Therefore, O thou son of man, speak unto the house of Israel; Thus ye speak, saying, If our transgressions and our sins be upon us, and we pine away in them, **how should we then live**?
>
> Say unto them, As I live, saith Yahweh God, I have no pleasure in the death of the wicked; but that the wicked turn from his way and live: turn ye, turn ye from your evil ways; for why will ye die, O house of Israel? (Ezekiel 33:10-11)

The way to live is to **turn from *evil ways***, i.e. "**wrong paths**." The nation as a whole is in for bad times. Pray that you can repent (change) and be spared. What is coming on the earth cannot be stopped, but you can escape, if you take heed.

Will you listen to what the word of God is saying, or will you tarry in the evil city because of unbelief? This is a cycle of Yahweh repeating itself. Scripture says, "And as it was in the days of Noe, so shall it be also in the days of the Son of man. They did eat, they drank, they married wives, they were given in marriage, until the day that Noe entered into the ark, and the flood came, and destroyed them all." (Luke 17:26-27; cf. Matthew 24:37-39).

Noah preached of the coming destruction for 120 years, and no one paid attention. He could not get one person to repent. Only his immediate family entered the ark with him. Are you listening now. We don't have 120 years left. Scientists are saying **the calamity is overdue. They give us anywhere from zero to fifty years, with a realistic likelihood of less than ten**.

Even if you do not believe the Bible, and you disregard all the Biblical and Bible Code evidence, there is still the overwhelming scientific data projecting the cycles of nature that must soon be fulfilled. These forces cannot be held back. You can put a cork in a steam kettle, but when the pressure builds, nothing can hold the cork in place. Yet the longer it waits to blow the harder it will pop. Nature is getting ready to pop.

If we want to find our way through this we need to repent.

JEWS AND CHRISTIANS UNITE

Our repentance or change does not limit itself to turning away from immoralities. It also refers to wrong religious beliefs. There are many good upstanding people in various religions, leading exemplary lives. Erroneous religious beliefs can hold us back spiritually. We are considering Christians and Jews, because they represent Israel and Judah who need to re-unite in the last days, in order to fulfill Scripture. Both must repent.

After the time of Solomon the tribes of Israel split into two groups, two separate nations, the House of Judah and the House of Israel. The true Jews are Judah, while the lost tribes of Israel have become Christian (encompassing all nationalities and races in both natural and spiritual Israel). The Old and New Testaments both say Judah and Israel will reunite in the last days. It seems impossible but it will happen.

Christians have generally made the mistake of rejecting everything Jewish, while Jews have rejected everything Christian.

Christians need to realize that the ten commandments were never dis-annulled and are as much in effect for them as they are for the Jews. We are not saved by keeping the commandments, but we can be lost by not keeping them.

Those who disregard the commandments are the "lawless ones" (2 Thessalonians 2:7-11).

Jews need to realize that our bodies are the temple, and that an earthly temple and reinstitution of animal sacrifice is not what God wants.

Scripture tells us, in the book of Hebrews, that Yesu is our great high priest ministering in the heavenly sanctuary for us. He is also the sacrificial lamb, "the Lamb of God that takes away the sin of the world." (John 1:29).

Jews must realize and confess that Yesu is Messiah. Re-institution of sacrificial offerings would be useless. God does not want animal blood. He only desires a humble heart.

> ...**to this man will I look, even to him that is poor and of a contrite spirit, and trembleth at my word**.
>
> He that killeth an ox is as if he slew a man; he that sacrificeth a lamb, as if he cut off a dog's neck; he that offereth an oblation, as if he offered swine's blood; he that burneth incense, as if he blessed an idol. Yea, they have chosen their own ways, and their soul delighteth in their abominations.
>
> (Isaiah 66:2-3).

Jews and Christians must both realize that Yahweh is Yesu, and Yesu is Yahweh, one God with many offices and manifestations; one God, one Spirit, and his name is important. No substitution will do.

HIS PEOPLE REBIRTHED

His name is closely related and attached to the new birth. When you are born of the water and the Spirit you are immersed into his name. When you are born of the Spirit your eyes are opened to the kingdom of God (see John 3:3-8).

Hear the word of Yahweh, **ye that tremble at his word**; **your brethren that hated you, that cast you out for my name's sake** [*because of my name*], said, Let Yahweh be glorified: but he shall appear to your joy, and they shall be ashamed.

A voice of noise from the city, a voice from the temple, a voice of Yahweh that rendereth recompence to his enemies.

Before she travailed, she brought forth; before her pain came, she was delivered of a man child.

Who hath heard such a thing? who hath seen such things? Shall the earth be made to bring forth in one day? or shall a nation be born at once? for as soon as Zion travailed, she brought forth her children.

Shall I bring to the birth, and not cause to bring forth? saith Yahweh: shall I cause to bring forth, and shut the womb? saith thy God.

(Isaiah 66:5-9).

It is time for the new birth for Jews and Christians alike, and anyone else who will receive the truth and repent/change.

In one of the Torah's hidden messages God has written in reverse, "**My people, surely you will rebirth**." The Hebrew word used here for "rebirth," also means, to *be reborn* or *resurrected*.

This amazing symmetrical Bible Code grid that encompasses the five books of the Torah, at a reverse skip of 19557, has the vertical search term phrase, "HaShem Yesu is verified/truth." To the Jew, HaShem is God. It is also a reference to the tetragrammaton, YHWH. This phrase can be read, "God is Yesu, is verified/truth," or, "Yahweh is Yesu, is verified/truth."

Literally HaShem means "the name." So the most literal rendering is, "The name of Yesu is verified/truth."

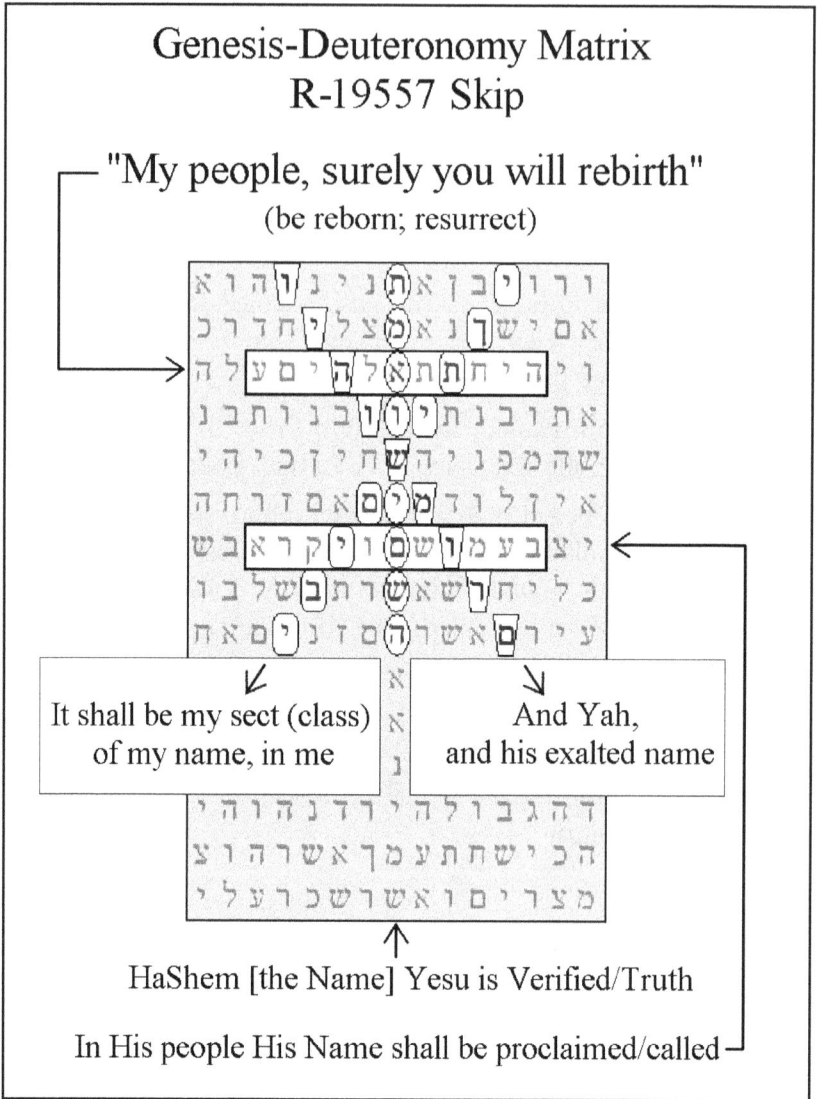

Genesis-Deuteronomy Matrix
R-19557 Skip

"My people, surely you will rebirth"
(be reborn; resurrect)

It shall be my sect (class) of my name, in me

And Yah, and his exalted name

HaShem [the Name] Yesu is Verified/Truth

In His people His Name shall be proclaimed/called

Biblecodes 2000

"My people, surely you will rebirth," is reversed from, "The terror of God was upon the cities." (Genesis 35:5).

Another horizontal line says, "In his people his name shall be proclaimed." Two diagonal phrases that cross in the middle say, "It shall be my sect (class) of my name, in me," "And Yah, and his exalted name." These are all statements verifying his name and the importance of it.

Genesis-Deuteronomy Matrix
R-19557 Skip

That class/genus of Abraham our Father:
HaShem [the Name] Yesu is Verified/Truth

נ י מ מ Classified; of class/genus [2x on diagonals]

Biblecodes 2000

A doubled *Aleph* is the Hebrew abbreviation for Abraham our Father. The complete central, vertical, key-phrase (at R-19557) states, "That class (genus) of Abraham our Father: HaShem Yesu is verified." It is like a DNA test verifying that Abraham is of the same line as HaShem-Yesu. "He [Yesu] took on him the seed of Abraham" (Hebrews 2:16). When we are *re-birthed* we are of that same line. "If ye be Christ's, then are ye Abraham's seed, and heirs according to the promise." (Galatians

3:29). Christ is of the genus of Abraham, and we are of his genus, i.e., his genetic code, his DNA. The word, "classified," or "from genus," appears twice, in symmetrical diagonals intersecting the *Mem* in HaShem-Yesu (previous chart).

Genesis-Deuteronomy Matrix
R-19557 Skip

Behold/Observe the teaching/learning/change
(reads the same in forward or reverse)

From the mountaintop →

↑ ↑ ↑
Behold the Ark | And Believe

HaShem [the Name] Yesu is Verified/Truth

Biblecodes 2000

Intersecting the name Yesu, at a 3-skip, is the perfectly symmetrical phrase, "Behold the teaching," or alternately,

"Observe the change." Forming an X over the central phrase, are the terms, "Behold (observe) the Ark," "And Believe." The Ark of the Covenant was a portal for the presence of God. Yesu manifests his presence in the New Covenant. He is the Ark, and the mediator between God and man, between the Spirit and the flesh. "From the mountaintop," is encoded in reverse. We are symbolically in the mountain of God when the Holy Spirit fills us. *From the mountaintop* may also have a literal fulfillment if we flee into the mountains to escape the coming events.

Genesis-Deuteronomy Matrix
R-19557 Skip

א ו ה ו נ ו ה י נ ת א ן נ ב י ו ר ו
כ ר ד ח י ל צ א נ ד ש י ס א
ה ל ע מ י ה ל ת ת ח י ה ו
ן ב ת ו נ ב ד ת נ ב ו ת א
י ה י כ ז ד י ח ה י נ פ מ ה ש
ה ח ר ז מ ס א ד ו ל י א
ש ב א ר ק ו ש מ ש ו ע מ ע ב צ י
ו ב ל ש ב ת ר ש א ר ח י ל כ
ח א ס י נ ז ה ר ש א ס מ ר י ע
ד י נ ב ל ת ו א מ ע ב ר א ו ן
ע מ ל ה א ל א מ ס ת א ח ק ל
א ר ת ו י ד ג נ ל ד ר ד ה ט ר
י ה ו ה נ ד ר י ה ל ו ב ג ה ד
צ ו ה ר ש א ך מ ע ת ח ש י כ ה
י ל ע ר כ ש ד ר ש א ו י מ ר צ מ

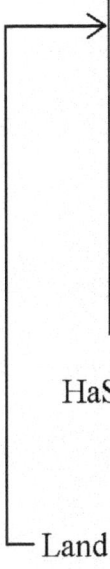

HaShem [the Name] Yesu is Verified/Truth

י ם ש י It shall be My Name

ו מ ש ו And His Name

Land of Israel [abbr י א] This is My Name

Crossing the name of Yesu, God states, "Land of Israel, This is my name." And he says, "It shall be my name," "and his name." That is the father and the son, the Spirit and the flesh. This encryption is reminiscent of Proverbs 30:4, "What is his name, and what is his son's name." This is not a two part God. God is one. This is simply a puzzle, an enigma, that becomes clear to those enlightened by the Holy Spirit. Yahweh, as Father, is telling the lost tribes (U.S.A.) that he is the *royal messenger* Yesu. He acts in both the capacities of father and son.

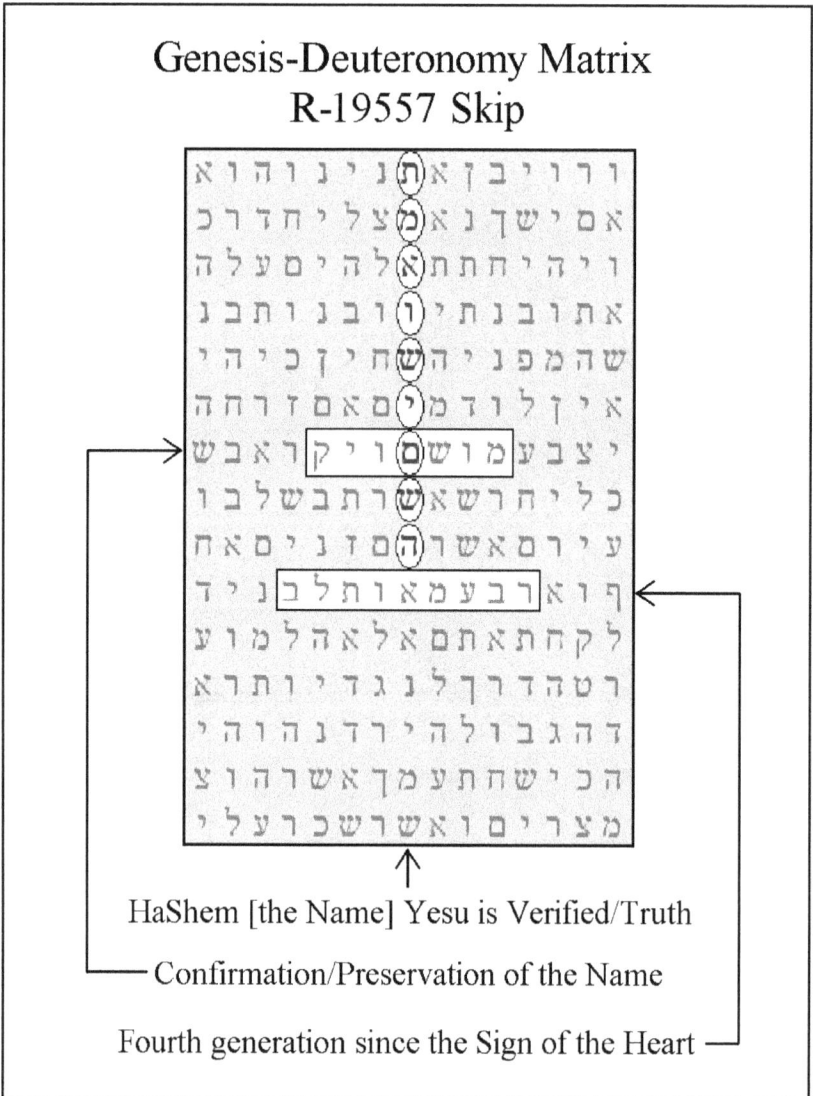

Genesis-Deuteronomy Matrix
R-19557 Skip

א ו ה י נ א (ת) נ י נ נ ב י ו ר ו
כ ר ד ח י ל צ א (מ) נ ד ש י ם א
ה ל ע ם ס י ה ל (א) ת ת ח י ה ה י ו
ן ב ת ו נ ב ו (ו) י ת נ ב ו ת א
י ה י כ ן י ח (ש) ה י נ פ מ ה ה ש
ה ח ר ז מ א ם (ם) מ ד ו ל ן י א
ש ב ר א ק י ו ש (ם) מ ע ב צ י
ו ב ל ש ב ת ר (ש) ר ח י ל כ
ע י ר ם א ש ר (ה) ם ס ז נ ס מ ר י א ח
ד י נ ל ת ו א מ ע ב ר א ו ף
ע ו מ ל ה א ל מ ת א ת ח ק ל
א ר ת ו י ד ג נ ל כ ר ד ד ה ט ר
י ה ו ה נ ד ר י ה ל ו ב ג ה ה ד
צ ו ה ר ש א ך מ ע ת ח ש י כ ה
י ל ע ר כ ש ר ש א ו מ י ר צ מ

HaShem [the Name] Yesu is Verified/Truth

Confirmation/Preservation of the Name

Fourth generation since the Sign of the Heart

The reversed code that says, "Confirmation/Preservation of the name," appears in the text of Exodus 34:5, where Yahweh came down to Moses in a cloud, to give the second set of commandments (after the first set had been smashed). The plain text says, "and he stood with him there and proclaimed the name of Yahweh." A symmetrical forward-code, superimposed on that phrase, says, "In his people his name shall be proclaimed/called." In the forward text he proclaims the name, in reverse he confirms and preserves it.

What is the significance of the phrase, "Fourth generation since the sign of the heart"? We may find the answer in God's own words, when he gave the commandments regarding his name, in chapter twenty of Exodus.

[1] And God spake all these words, saying,

[2] I am Yahweh thy God, which have brought thee out of the land of Egypt, out of the house of bondage.

[3] Thou shalt have no other gods before me.

[4] Thou shalt not make unto thee any graven image, or any likeness of any thing that is in heaven above, or that is in the earth beneath, or that is in the water under the earth:

[5] Thou shalt not bow down thyself to them, nor serve them: for I Yahweh thy God am a jealous God, **visiting the *fault* of the fathers upon the children unto the third and *fourth generation* for** *altering/changing* (לשׂנאי) **me** [*translated from Hebrew text; cf. Strongs #8133*];

[6] And shewing mercy unto thousands of them that love me, and keep my commandments.

[7] Thou shalt not take **the name of Yahweh** thy God in vain; for **Yahweh** will not hold him guiltless (*not acquit him*) that taketh his name in vain.

The English speaking people have altered him by changing his name. Therefore they are taking his name in vain. Forgiveness of sin is in the name of Yesu-Yahweh. When his name is taken in vain by calling out a counterfeit, and baptizing in an erroneous name, there is no acquittal. If the sign of the heart was when Yesu (Iesu) was changed to Jesus, in 1776, and a generation is seventy years, we are now living in the "Fourth generation since the sign of the heart." This is the time that the iniquity or fault of our fathers is to be lifted. This is evident in the fact that the the name change has been revealed to us, and the true names restored to their authenticity. Now we can be acquitted in the name of Yesu who is Yahweh our Saviour.

In the big picture, if the damage to New York is even a small fraction of what has been predicted, it has the potential of being one of the greatest disasters ever to plague the Earth. When the heart of the nation is damaged it affects the entire nation. The severity of the damage will determine whether the whole nation will crumble or survive.

In the coming disaster we have not even considered terrorism. If terrorists strike while the nation is in turmoil the additional devastation will be unbearable.

These are my research findings from countless hours of diligent study, but don't just take my word for anything, check it all out yourself. Do some of your own investigation. Don't believe it because I have said it, rather believe it because you have thoroughly investigated and weighed the evidence yourself. "Study to show thyself approved." Then if you feel you are in danger, do what you think you must. **If you choose to move to another area do it strictly because that is what you have decided is best and because you feel that it is the right thing to do.** It may save your life.

The judgment that is bearing down on the U.S. right now is in a great part a recompense for what we have done to God's name. *Who changed God's name* will explain exactly what has happened, how and why it happened, as well as what must be done about it.

May your eyes be opened.

THE END IS COME

BOOK 2

WHO CHANGED GOD'S NAME?

YESU CONFIRMED IN THE CODES

The name of Yesu is recorded countless times in the Bible Codes with both spellings (יֵשׁוּ and יֵשׁוּעַ) viewed as identical, which confirms the Yesu pronunciation.

One of these particularly significant codes is written at a matrix skip of -53812, within the section of Scripture between Leviticus 10: 4, through 1Chronicles 16: 30. The minus code indicates that it is written in reverse.

Hebrew is read from right to left, and begins at what we would consider the back of the book, but in Hebrew is actually the front. When we speak of a reverse skip in a Bible Code it means that instead of reading from right to left, as Hebrew normally is, we read from left to right. In other words, it begins at the back of the Bible and goes toward the front. This is very significant, because God tells us in Scripture, that he sees the end from the beginning. When we pick up a Hebrew Bible and hold it like any other book, we are looking at the back of the Bible, seeing the end of it first. In other words, seeing the end from the beginning. So a code written in reverse may be symbolic of how God sees things before they happen. To him it is already written and has already taken place.

This -53812 code confirms the name of Yesu in the two Hebrew spellings. They are each pronounced exactly the same.

מוותתעמובהרנחלתכמכונלשבתכ
אמשהאלמישאלואלאלצפנבניעזי
יהמהרוחויתנבאוולאיספוויישא
בכפניחרהאפיהוהאלהיכבכוהשמ
לכואלהמארדבוישובינביתאלוב
אותאתמפלתהאריההונהנהעדתדבור
דלשאוללמהתתשמעאתדבריאדמלאמ
ותהילמלכסכנתותשרתהווהמלכל
לכוישלחאליהוהושפטמלכיהודהלא
ריולאישמחאדנוואתיתמיוואתא
כאיהקנאתכוגבורתכהמונמעיכו
עריההרובעריהשפלהובעריהנגב
תבנילכגבותעשלכרמהבכלרחוב
תוכוהתרומהאשרתרימולייהוהאר
להמאדומשחציההרדצפונהוחציון
יהלכמקטבישודשהרימימפלמצדכא
תדלימכסאולעדיכונשבטותוכחת
עותרוחושבתיאניוארההבלתתחת
תאלהשמיאדילמהלהואקצפעלמלכ
דשחילומלפניובלהארצאפתכונת
תגרהברעהונפלתאתהויהודהעמכ

Central Key-Phrase confirms the name of Yesu in both spellings

"Priest of new fresh olive oil: Yesu is Yesu(a); Yesu is of Abraham our Father"

(Codefinder Matrix skip, -53812. Leviticus 10: 4, through 1Chronicles 16: 30)

Term	Translation	Skip	R Factor	Start	End
בהן יצהר ישו ישוע ישואא	Priest of new fresh olive oil: Yesu is Yesu(a); Yesu is of Abraham our Father.	-53812	11.353	1 Chronicles 16:30.11	Leviticus 10:4.17
האריהוה	The Lion exists	1	-0.301	Judges 14:8.30	Judges 14:8.36
משיח	He shall be the Messiah	-3	-0.946	2 Kings 3:7.21	2 Kings 3:7.9
חבבןוען	Your bosom is the anchor	-4	2.160	Ezekiel 16:24.24	Ezekiel 16:24.4
בישודצהרימי	In Yesu rejoice, o' mountain of my sea.	1	0.000	Psalms 91:6.16	Psalms 91:7.1

The ELS reference is 53812 characters between rows.
There are 5 displayed terms in the matrix.
The matrix starts at Leviticus 10:4.7 and ends at 1 Chronicles 16:30.21.
The matrix spans 968637 characters of the surface text.
The matrix has 19 rows, is 21 columns wide and contains a total of 399 characters.
There are 5 significant terms in the matrix.
The matrix odds are 1 chance in 1.49369522748572E26 in favour of significance.
The cumulative 'R' Factor for the displayed matrix is 26.174.

The 'R' Factor is used in both the Term Identification and the Matrix Report features of CodeFinder. It is a number derived from the logarithm of the reciprocal of the expected number of occurrences of the selected term at +/- the skip distance it was found at. In simple terms a negative number indicates decreasing significance whilst a positive number indicates increasing significance, zero would show that the odds were 1:1 of the term occurring at the skip distance that it was found at.

A term with an 'R' Factor of 8 only has a 1:100,000,000 chance of occurring at the skip it was found at. Conversely, a term with an 'R' Factor of -2 would be expected to have about 100 occurrences within the skip range that it was found in.

Note that the 'R' Factor is derived from the entire text that the term was found in, not from just the area covered by the matrix.

Codefinder report: Leviticus 10: 4, through 1Chronicles 16: 30, Matrix skip, -53812.

Name of Yesu same in both spellings: "Priest of new fresh olive oil: Yesu is Yesu(a); Yesu is of Abraham our Father" 1 chance in 225,519,586,986 in favor of significance.

The three letter spelling is ישו, and the four letter spelling is ישוע. They are displayed here in English as Yesu and Yesu(a). Both spellings are pronounced Yesu (variant, Yeshu). The (a) represents the silent letter *Ayin*, and is shown here only to indicate the presence of the four-letter spelling. It is not pronounced Yeshua. Usually the *Ayin* is represented by `, and the name would appear as Yesu`, or Yeshu`. Showing it here as Yesu(a) is to indicate that when you see the erroneous rendering Yeshua, the *a* is not to be pronounced.

The key phrase, **"Priest of new fresh olive oil: Yesu is Yesu(a); Yesu is of Abraham our Father,"** is found at -53812 skip (- indicates reversed code). For this term alone in the matrix, odds are 1 chance in 225,519,586,986 in favor of significance (*Codefinder* report). That means there is only one chance in over 225 billion for this sentence to appear randomly in the Bible text.

The phrase is reproduced here in normal Hebrew, right to left, so that it can easily be read by Hebrew speaking people:

כהן יצהר ישו ישוע ישו אא

This sentence is totally relevant to Yesu's position as outlined in the plain text of Scripture, both in Old Testament and New, and confirms the validity and accuracy of fulfilled prophecy as recorded in the open text of the Bible. A "Priest of new fresh olive oil," signifies his anointed position as Messiah, as well as his initiating of the "gift" of the Holy Spirit, which would anoint his followers. The אא, is the Hebrew abbreviation for Abraham our Father. "Yesu is of Abraham our Father," is a response to the Bible verses in John 8: 51-58.

> Verily, verily, I say unto you, If a man keep my saying, he shall never see death.
>
> Then said the Jews unto him, Now we know that thou hast a devil. Abraham is dead, and the prophets; and thou sayest, If a man keep my saying, he shall never taste of death.
>
> Art thou greater than our father Abraham, which is dead? and the prophets are dead: whom makest thou thyself?
>
> Yesu answered, If I honour myself, my honour is nothing: it is my Father that honoureth me; of whom ye say, that he is your God:
>
> Your father Abraham rejoiced to see my day: and he saw it, and was glad.
>
> Then said the Jews unto him, Thou art not yet fifty years old, and hast thou seen Abraham?
>
> Yesu said unto them, Verily, verily, I say unto you, Before Abraham was, I am.

They ridiculed Yesu for saying that he had been with Abraham our father. The Torah Code confirms that he was, by stating, "Yesu is of Abraham our Father."

Along with the key term, "Priest of new fresh olive oil: Yesu is Yesu(a); Yesu is of Abraham our Father," are four other significant phrases encoded symmetrically. In sequential order from top to bottom they are, "The Lion exists," "He shall be the

Messiah," "Your bosom is the anchor," and, "In Yesu, rejoice, O' mountain of my sea."

The phrase "He shall be the Messiah," is a second reference to his being the Anointed ("of new fresh olive oil") in this grid.

"The Lion exists," refers to Yesu as the Lion of the Tribe of Judah. A detail of the grid shows, האְרי הוה, *the Lion exists*, intersected at front and back by, הוה, *to be, to exist*, like two legs rising up to support another, הוה, with a center pillar of יׁשו, Yesu. The word הוה, appears four times interconnected in this tiny grid. The הוה, to be/exist, is part of the name of Yahweh, יהוה, he will be, or, "He will exist." The name Yesu, יׁשו, translates literally, "His existence," viz. He Exists, his earthly manifestation. Yesu also means, Yahweh the Saviour, or, Yahweh is Salvation. Yahweh is Yesu thus salvation in Yahweh is salvation in Yesu.

מ י ש א ל ו א ל א ל צ פ נ
ח ו י ת נ ב א ו ו ל א י ס
ר ה א פ י ה ו ה א ל ה י כ
מ א ר ד ב ו י ש ב ו ב י נ ב
פ ל ת ה א ר י ה ו ה נ ה ע
ל מ ה ת ש מ ע א ת ד ב ר י
ל כ ס כ נ ת ו ת ש ר ת ה ו

"The Lion exists; Yesu; exists; exists; exists"

(Detail of -53812 matrix, Leviticus 10: 4, through 1Chronicles 16: 30)

"Your bosom is the anchor," is a metaphor of salvation in Yesu. In ancient times the Anchor was a symbol of safety, and relates to the hope of salvation. The Apostle Paul said, we have hope of our soul anchored within the vail, where Yesu has entered for us as high priest forever, after the order of the Righteous King (Hebrews 6: 18-20). His bosom is our anchor in the heavenly tabernacle.

The final word cluster states, "In Yesu, rejoice, o' mountain of my sea." A mountain is symbolic of a kingdom. "My sea," is the Sea of Truth, the Torah. Sea is also a Biblical metaphor for people. His people of the truth, of the Torah, are the Sea of Truth and his living word. *Rejoice in Yesu, O' kingdom of my people.*

JUST ONE NAME

Proverbs 30: 4, says, "Who hath ascended up into heaven, or descended? who hath gathered the wind in his fists? who hath bound the waters in a garment? who hath established all the ends of the earth? **what is his name, and what is his son's name, if thou canst tell**?"

In a 23-skip grid the name Yesu intersects this phrase three times, symmetrically (see **Chart 1**). When the letters in this phrase are limited to a symmetrical cluster, the line reads, "**A piece** [*of the puzzle*] **what is his name and what is his son's name?**" The Hebrew word רץ (*ratz*) means a *fragment* or *piece*. This suggests a piece of a puzzle in which the whole has been fragmented and we must re-assemble the pieces to see the picture. The puzzle is, "what is his name, and what is his son's name." The term "and Yesu," appears twice, on symmetrical diagonals. First, on the right, Yesu crosses through "the name of him." The second time, Yesu crosses through "the name of his son." This indicates that both names are the same one name. The Father and Son are Yesu.

The Hebrew word רץ (*ratz*) also means a "royal messenger" (p.315, *Pocket Hebrew Dictionary*, Langenscheidt). Thus an alternate reading is, "**The royal messenger, what is his name and what is his son's name?**"

In the central column the name Yesu appears again, in what looks like a 3-skip, starting from bottom and counting up. In actuality it is a 69-skip sequence, meaning that if you count the number of letters (to the left) until you arrive at the next letter in the name it will be 69. Since we are looking at a grid with 23 letters in each line it takes three laps to reach the next letter, totaling a 69-skip count.

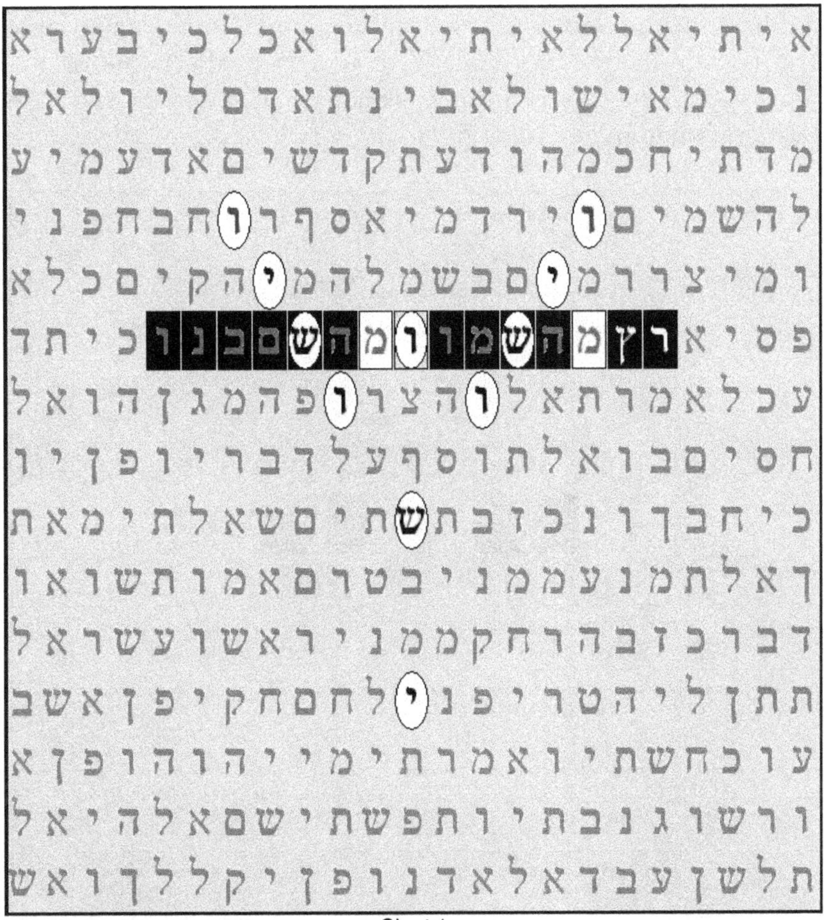

Chart 1
A Piece, What is His Name and What is His Son's Name
(Proverbs 30: 1-10; Biblecodes 2000)

Upon closer examination we see the Hebrew term HaShem (השם) crossing the name Yesu in both of the diagonals (**Chart 2**). Modern Hebrew script has five letters that each have a *sof*, or ending form, different than the initial (ך=כ, ם=מ, ן=נ, ף=פ, ץ=צ). In these word clusters, HaShem uses the two examples of *Mem* (השם and השם). These are both forms of the same letter M. The Bible Code treats them as identical because virtually there is no difference, somewhat like in English, M and m are the same letter.

HaShem means "the Name." It is also an Hebrew appellation for the Tetragrammaton, YHWH. To the Jew, HaShem means God, and is so translated in Hebrew dictionaries. In this code matrix the name Yesu is seen as the name of the father and the son, and is equated with God and the Tetragrammaton.

Chart 2
HaShem and Yesu; HaShem and Yesu
(Proverbs 30: 1-10; Biblecodes 2000)

In the next view of this matrix (**Chart 3**) we see the Hebrew phrase מֶשֶׁת, *meshat*, which translates, "from the foundation." This could mean, from the foundation of God's creation, of which Yesu was there from the foundation, or it could mean the foundation stone, of which Yesu is that stone. Since Yesu and Yahweh are one there is no difference. The term *meshat*, appears twice, symmetrically. It crosses through Yesu and HaShem in both places, on the right and on the left, indicating that the father and the son are One from the foundation. (Again we see the two forms of *Mem*, the *sof* and initial, משת, משת).

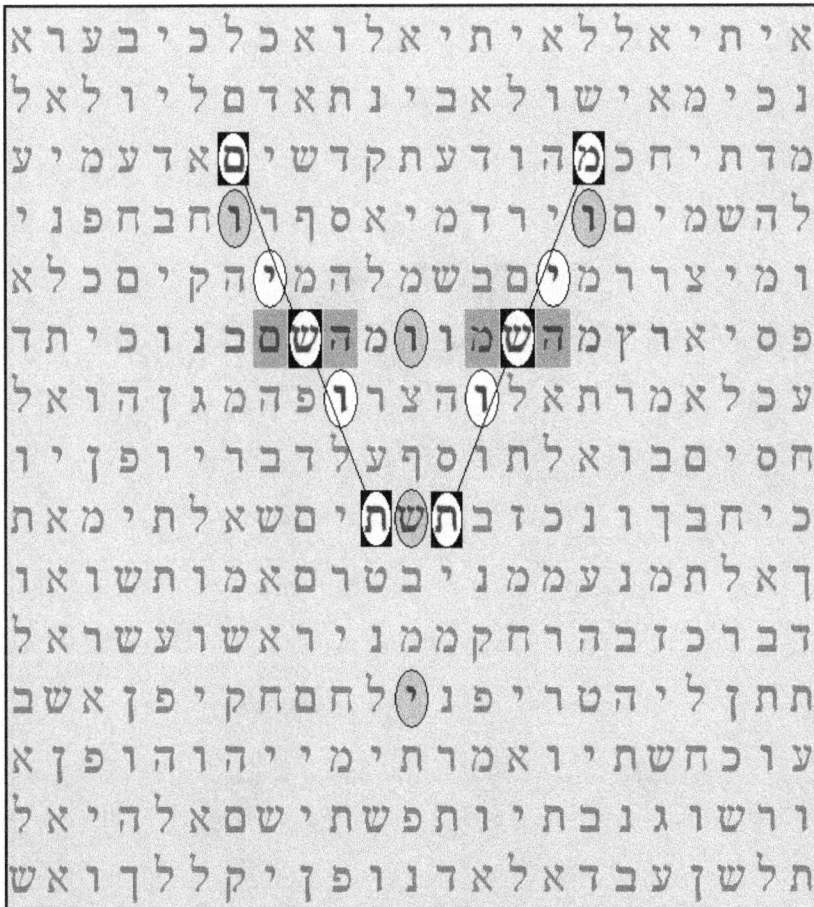

Chart 3
MeShat HaShem Yesu; MeShat HaShem Yesu
(Proverbs 30: 1-10; Biblecodes 2000)

We have seen two symmetrical clusters of *Yesu, HaShem, from the foundation*, and the first horizontal line, "A piece [*of the puzzle*] what is his name and what is his son's name?" with the alternate reading, "The royal messenger, what is his name and what is his son's name?"

Further symmetrical deciphering of Proverbs 30: 1-13, in **Chart 4**, brings to light some of the operational mechanics of Yahweh's hidden code.

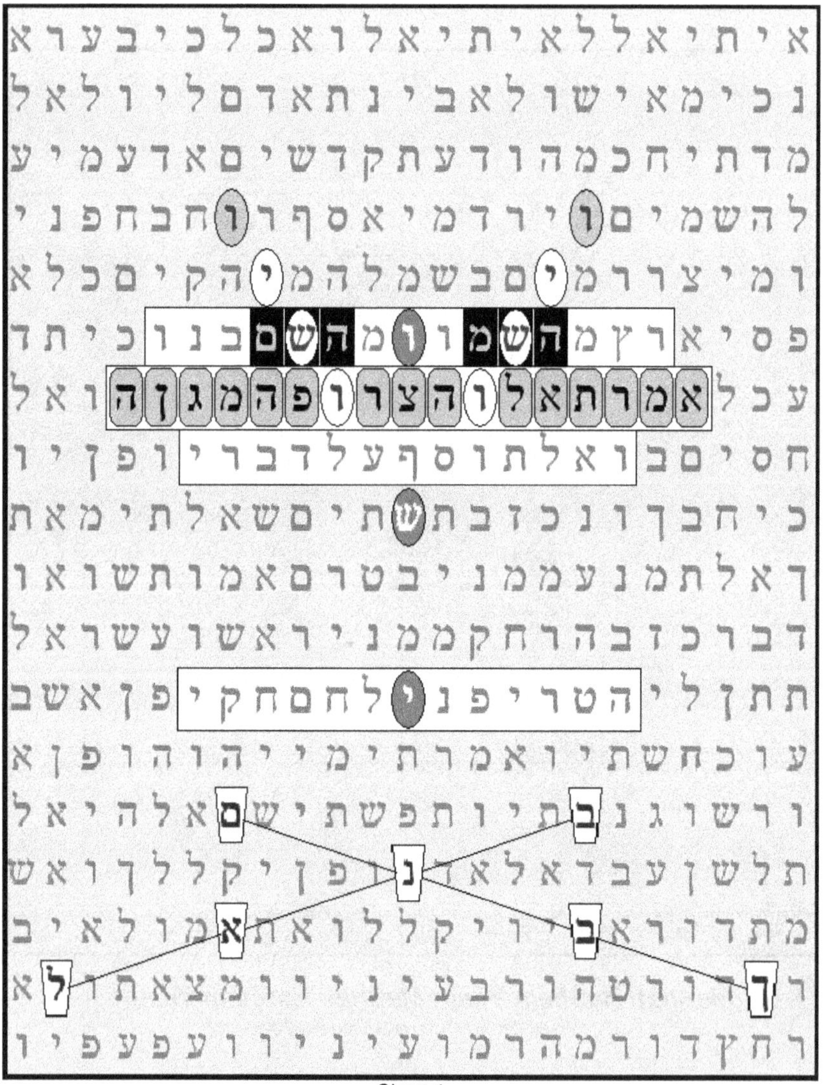

Chart 4
An Acrostic Shield
(Proverbs 30: 1-13; Biblecodes 2000)

The second line in **Chart 4** can read, "The word of God is a tested shield," or "The word of God is a refined covering/shield." The word *covering* is from מגנה (מגּזְה) which also means "blindness" (p. 164, *Pocket Hebrew Dictionary*, Langenscheidt). This indicates that Scripture is a shield to blind those not meant to see, in fulfillment of the prophecy of Isaiah 6: 9-10.

This same line can read, "The word of God is an acrostic covering." The word translated, "tested/refined/purified," צרופה, also means "joining," or "fusion." This describes the word of God and the Code. The same word is also translated "acrostic" (*Ben Yehuda's English-Hebrew/Hebrew-English Pocket Dictionary*, p. 261). Thus, the phrase can read, "The word of God is an acrostic covering," or, "The word of God is an acrostic shield." This confirms that his word is a puzzle. An acrostic is a word or phrase made up of initials of other meaningful words. This happens in the codes.

The third horizontal line is, ואל תו סף על דברי, "Don't mark the end (*sof*) on my word." This seems to be saying exactly what code researchers have realized from the start, that the *sof*, or ending letters are to be treated the same as initials, in other words, a *sof* letter does not indicate the end of a word in the code. Some of the code programs have changed the *sof* letters back to their original forms. **The first Scriptures were written without space between words and without punctuation. Neither did they have any diacritical points for added vowels. The Holy Spirit could inspire a reader to see and read the letters in various clusters, thus rendering alternate readings.** Separating of the letters in different places it would change the meaning and content of the sentence. One line of letters could be read in several different ways each time conveying a new meaning. As long as no *sof* letters were used a forced ending would not occur.

God, in the beginning, the Source, is called *Ain (Ein) Sof*, "no end," or "without end." Is there any wonder he would not want an end marked on his words?

This line that says, "Don't mark the end (*sof*) on my word," in its entirety in plain text Scripture, says, "Add thou not

unto his words, lest he reprove thee, and thou be found a liar."
(Proverbs 30:6).

By adding *sof* letters, separating words, punctuating and
adding vowel points, they changed his word and locked it into
one mode of interpretation, limiting what God could say through
his written word. Ancient Jewish mystics ignored these devices so
they could read the Scriptures and decipher hidden meanings.
Through the Bible Code we are now rediscovering this lost key of
reading the word of Yahweh.

The fourth horizontal cluster shown in this Acrostic Shield
grid matrix, חקי להם פני הטרי, says, "The new face of the
bread is my statute." This is a direct reference to the New
Covenant.

> Then Yesu said unto them, Verily,
> verily, I say unto you, Moses gave you
> not that bread from heaven; but my
> Father giveth you the true bread from
> heaven. For the bread of God is he
> which cometh down from heaven, and
> giveth life unto the world. Then said
> they unto him, Lord, evermore give us
> this bread. And Yesu said unto them, I
> am the bread of life: he that cometh to
> me shall never hunger; and he that
> believeth on me shall never thirst.
> (John 6: 32-35).

Beneath the fourth horizontal cluster we see two phrases
crossed in an X. The one sloping to the left, אל בנ (בן אל) says,
"Son of God." The one sloping to the right, בך סנ (מן בך) says,
"Manna in you." There it is, the bread of the New Covenant, the
Word of God in you. "It is written, Man shall not live by bread
alone, but by every word that proceedeth out of the mouth of
God." (Matthew 4: 4).

"The new face of the bread is my statute."

HIS NAME AND HIS SON'S NAME
HIS NAME AND HIS FATHER'S NAME

Consider Proverbs 30:4, and Revelation 14:1. He marks 144,000.
They will be marked with a name that belongs to the father and son.

Yahweh is the name of the Father, as the invisible Spirit. He said, "Beside me there is no Saviour" (Isaiah 43:11). He was manifested to the world as Yesu Christ. There is salvation in no other (Acts 4:12). The Son is the physical manifestation of the Spirit/Father. Yahweh is the Saviour. The name Yesu means *Yahweh the Saviour*, and from the Hebrew it is literally translated, "His existence." Yesu and Yahweh are one. The translation of Yahweh is, "He will be;" Yesu is, "His existence," essentially, "*He is*." Whether we say Yahweh or Yesu, we are speaking of the one same Saviour. His name is his mark.

THE NAME OF YESU IS AUTHENTIC

At a reverse skip of 21,381, in a matrix encompassing Genesis through Numbers, the key-phrase that appears is, "The name of Yesu is authentic." Two other phrases form a perfect X through it. An I with an X through it is a symbol of the initials of Yesu Christ, from the Greek, IX, for *Iesou Xristou.*

The first of the terms forming the X is, "Alas! Yesu HaNotzr." *Ha* is "the," *Notzr* (נוֹצֵר) נוצר is "watchman." The statement says, "Alas! Yesu the Watchman." The Jews will recognize this term since it is unmistakably close to the title *Yesu HaNotzry*, by which they refer to Christ; and *Notzry* means "*my watchman*." The other term in the X is, "What a debt that is heaped up."

The three sentences comprising the IX monogram of *Iesou Xristou* (Yesu Christ) are,

The name of Yesu is authentic.

Alas! Yesu HaNotzr (the Watchman).

What a debt that is heaped up.

The verses that run through this matrix grid are, from top line, to bottom, Genesis 23:20; 34:30; 47:4; Exodus11:3; 25:33; 38:1-2; Leviticus 12:2; 24:12; Numbers 7:47; 19:20.

Each line in the expanded matrix would be 21,381 letters long. We are only viewing a small portion here, cropped from the larger grid. To find such an extensive code in a grid of just 130 letters is extremely significant.

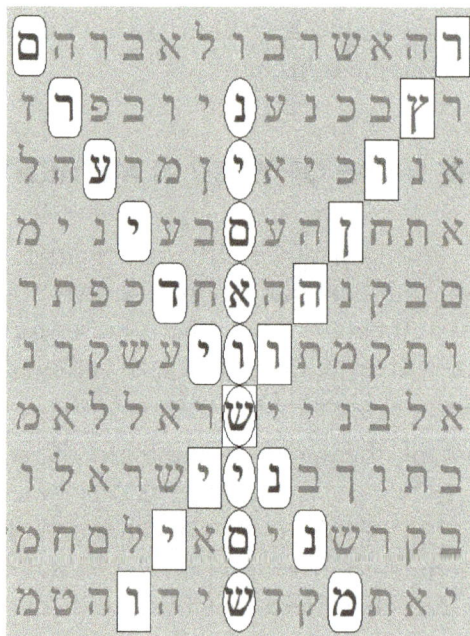

Genesis-Numbers Matrix
R-21381 Skip

The name of Yesu
is authentic

Alas! Yesu HaNotzr/the Watchman

What a debt that is heaped up

WATCHMAN'S WARNING

Yesu is the watchman of Israel. He came unto his own, 2,000 years ago, to show the way and clear the debt. When he was rejected by the Jews he then reached out to the lost sheep of the House of Israel. Many of the Jews had rejected and scorned him at that time, and he is continually scorned today, so that *the debt is heaped up* (מננשידיערם, for, מן נשי די ערם = "What a debt that is heaped up").

It is time to heed the watchman's warning. We are now living in the day of judgment. It is time to make some changes or be taken away in God's wrath.

The same Hebrew word for Christians, literally means means Watchmen. It is derived from *Yesu HaNotzry*: "Yesu my watchman."

Notzr (נוצר) means watchman (singular). With a *yod* suffix, *notzry* (נוצרי) can be taken to mean either, "watchmen," or "my watchman," but is also the word for Christian.

Christians, as Israelites, are supposed to be God's watchmen. Yesu is the Watchman. True Christians, as the Body of Christ, are an extension of Yesu and his attributes in this world. Thus, the Body of Christ is the watchman, so all true Christians are watchmen.

As one of his watchmen of the last days, Yahweh has set me on a mission to share the light he has revealed.

So thou, O son of man, I have set thee a watchman *unto the house of Israel*; therefore **thou shalt hear the word at my mouth, and warn them from me**. (Ezekiel 33:7)

Therefore, O thou son of man, speak unto the house of Israel; Thus ye speak, saying, If our transgressions and our sins be upon us, and we pine away in them, **how should we then live**?

Say unto them, As I live, saith Yahweh God, I have no pleasure in the death of the wicked; but that the wicked turn from his way and live: turn

ye, turn ye from your evil ways; for why will ye die,
O house of Israel? (Ezekiel 33:10-11).

Ezekiel's warning is being sounded to call together into one people the true Jews and the scattered Israelites (wherever and whoever they may be) who will hearken to the call to listen and to hear what the Holy Spirit is saying through the Scriptures. The two rods must grow together and re-unite in the last days (see, Ezekiel 37:16-22).

Yahweh-Yesu is calling together the lost sheep of the House of Israel and Judah to make them one flock.

> As the Father knoweth me, even so know I the Father: and I lay down my life for the sheep.
>
> And other sheep I have, which are not of this fold: them also I must bring, and they shall hear my voice; and there shall be one fold, and one shepherd.
>
> Therefore doth my Father love me, because I lay down my life, that I might take it again.
>
> (John 17:15-17).

The Jewish high priest Caiaphas understood this was the destiny of Yesu. He knew, through the Scriptures, that Yesu was the Messiah who would by his death, bring the lost sheep back together in the end. Not only was it preordained according to the Torah, but Caiaphas, himself, had prophesied it by the power of the Holy Spirit.

> And one of them, named Caiaphas, being the high priest that same year, said unto them, Ye know nothing at all,
>
> nor consider that it is expedient for us, that one man should die for the people, and that the whole nation perish not.
>
> And this spake he not of himself: but being high priest that year, **he prophesied that Yesu should die for that nation;**
>
> **And not for that nation only, but that also he should gather together in one the children of God that were scattered abroad.**

Then from that day forth they took counsel together for
to put him to death.

(John 11:49-53).

This was all part of God's plan and had to be accomplished to
fulfill Scripture.

Genesis-Numbers Matrix
R-21381 Skip

The perfect Holy (temple/sanctuary) of Yahweh ⌐

Lamenting from A.I. (א Land of Israel) ────

Mediator of the Children of Israel ──────

The lamenting of Israel ────────

"The name of Yesu is authentic"

There are yet more symmetrical codes within the 21,381-skip Authentic Name grid.

Crossing directly through the initial *Yod* in the name of Yesu, is the phrase, "Mediator of the Children of Israel," and crossing through the letter *Shin* in his name is the statement, "The lamenting of Israel."

Two additional terms are marked here. One is, "Lamenting from the Land of Israel." (Land of Israel is the accepted lexicon abbreviation, אֵי, *ai*). The other says, "The perfect Holy (temple/sanctuary) of Yahweh." This was precisely Yesu's position. He was the temple or tabernacle of God in our midst. When he fills us with the Holy Spirit, we become the temple. "Know ye not that ye are the temple of God, and that the Spirit of God dwelleth in you?" (1Corinthians 3:16).

"What? know ye not that your body is the temple of the Holy Ghost which is in you, which ye have of God, and ye are not your own?" (1Corinthians 6:19).

In Ezekiel 37, when Yahweh-Yesu promised the Israelites he would put his sanctuary "*in the midst* of them," the Hebrew word he used was, בתוך (beTOKH) "inside." His sanctuary inside of them. The sanctuary is the Holy of Holies in the Temple.

> Moreover **I will make a covenant of peace** with them; it shall be **an everlasting covenant** with them: and I will place them, and multiply them, **and will set my sanctuary inside of them** for evermore.
>
> My tabernacle also shall be with them: yea, I will be their God, and they shall be my people.
>
> And the heathen shall know that I Yahweh do sanctify Israel, when **my sanctuary shall be inside of them** for evermore.
>
> (Ezekiel 37:26-28)

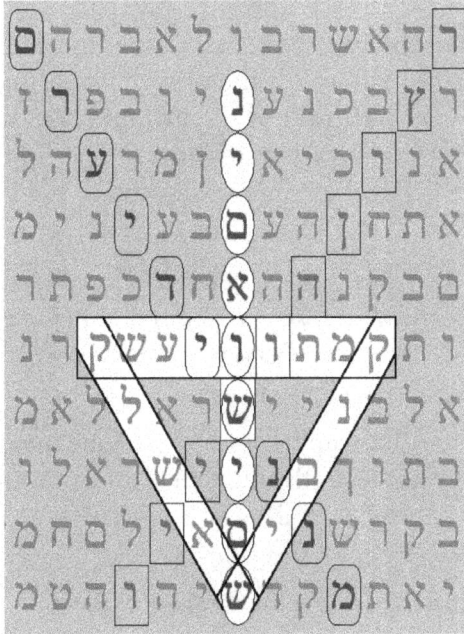

Genesis-Numbers Matrix
R-21381 Skip

[They] trim down the substance | [They] water down the fire

The name of Yesu is authentic

The enemy of His mark shall quarrel

Bible Codes 2000

A further analysis of the authentic name grid produces an inverted triangle of interlocking phrases superimposed symmetrically upon the key-statement, "The name of Yesu is authentic." The top line, going through the letter *waw* in his name, says, "The enemy of his mark shall quarrel." The same word for *mark* is also *cross* (p. 367, *ibid.* Langenscheidt). An equally accurate rendering of the phrase is, "**The enemy of his cross shall quarrel**."

In Ezekiel 9:4, Yahweh's chosen are sealed in the forehead with his mark. Some scholars say it is a cross. Revelation 7:3-4 gives us the same scenario. Later we are told that his mark is "his name and his Father's name," as referenced in Revelation 14:1, of the Greek New Testament transcripts.

We have already seen that his name and his Father's name are the same. Yahweh is the only Saviour, and Yesu means Yahweh the Saviour. Yahweh is the first and last; Yesu is the first and last. Do not try to separate them. Yesu said, "I and my Father are One." His mark is his name and his Father's name, Yesu.

Traditionally, Jews have rejected Yesu. They are *enemies of his mark*, and *enemies of his cross*, i.e. the redemption he bought with his blood. This is only because they have not yet been enlightened.

Lost Israel, basically English speaking people, have also become *enemies of his mark*, through the distortion of his name by the destruction of his *Yod*. This also is because they have not been enlightened.

"The enemy of his mark shall quarrel," is probably a reference to the reaction of those who will continue to refuse the truth. Although it is laid out right before their eyes, they will continue to argue about it and reject it.

Connected to this phrase on the diagonals are the terms, "*They* trim down the substance," and, "*They* water down the fire." These are two obvious references to the downplaying the importance of the names Yahweh and Yesu. Watering down the fire may be a reference to *quenching the Holy Spirit*.

We have found these ten highly significant terms encoded symmetrically within the tiny matrix of 130 letters:

"The name of Yesu is authentic."

"The enemy of his mark/cross shall quarrel."

"*They* trim down the substance."

"*They* water down the fire."

"Alas! Yesu (*HaNotzi*) the Watchman."

"What a debt that is heaped up."

"Mediator of the Children of Israel."

"The lamenting of Israel."

"Lamenting from the Land of Israel."

"The perfect Holy (temple/sanctuary) of Yahweh."

These ten phrases, apparently prophetic of end times, far from exhaust the possibilities for deciphering and exegesis of this small portion of the 21,381-skip matrix. The 130 letter grid holds many additional codes in itself, while the entire matrix would reach far beyond comprehension.

Codes of the end times exist beyond measure throughout the Hebrew Scriptures, virtually recording all things.

UNFORGETTING THE FORGOTTEN

THE FORGOTTEN NAME

But I was like a lamb or an ox that is brought to the slaughter; and I knew not that they had devised devices against me, saying, Let us destroy the tree with the fruit thereof, and let us cut him off from the land of the living, **that his name may be no more remembered.** (Jeremiah 11:19)

How long shall this be in the heart of the prophets that prophesy lies? yea, they are prophets of the deceit of their own heart; Which think to **cause my people to forget my name**... (Jeremiah 23:26-27)

You are about to learn the secrets of the "forgotten" name, and how its gradual distortion spawned an illegitimate counterfeit to deceive the very elect (cf. Matthew 24:24). The Key of knowledge was removed so that the compound name of God and Saviour could secretly be removed from common use without raising suspicion or inciting controversy. By gradually replacing the name(s) one bit at a time, during a period in which the early English language was in a state of adolescent confusion, with inconsistencies in the spellings of many words, no one ever realized what had happened.

IS EARTH STILL HERE

"Till heaven and earth pass, one jot [Hebrew, **yod** =Y] or one tittle shall in no wise pass from the law [Hebrew, **Torah**], till all be fulfilled." (Matthew 5:18). We have a heavenly promise that as long as Earth is still here not one letter *yod* has been removed from the Hebrew Scriptures, so the Saviour's name is still in tact. We have no such promise of Bibles in the vernacular, like English translations.

THE MASSES HAVE BEEN DECEIVED

Modern Christianity has been duped. Without ever knowing it, the Antichrist that they are warning against has already infiltrated the "Church." The literal meaning of Antichrist is "Instead of Christ." Many Christians have unwittingly and unknowingly become servants to the Antichrist. This sounds like a harsh statement, but you will soon understand how sadly true it is.

The original Biblical name of Yesu (Iesu) was changed to Jesus less than 300 years ago within the English speaking nations. The name of Yahweh underwent a more gradual metamorphosis, beginning about 200 years earlier, resulting in the spurious hybrid name Jehovah. Modern man has come to believe that Jesus and Jehovah are legitimate names for God and Saviour, when in reality they are newly formed from "strange slips" (cf. Isaiah 17:10). Yesu and Yahweh are names given from heaven, so closely related as to be interchangeable in Scripture. Jesus and Jehovah are counterfeit names invented by man, and distorted by the language of the end-time Babylon.

The following treatise is part of a documented research study into the historical linguistic changes in the names of God and Saviour, from the oldest known manuscripts to the modern present-day English versions of the Bible. The following excerpts are revised and updated from *Six Nights Till Morning: The Real Star Wars*, Chapter 19, "Who Changed God's Name?" (Selected pages 541-588, Copyright 1983, 1984, 2003, 2006, by Norbert H. Kox).

THERE IS NO HEBREW JEHOVAH

The modern name for God most commonly used is Jehovah, yet this name does not appear even once in the original Hebrew Scriptures. This is not the name, which was given by God to the Israelites. Jehovah is a misnomer.

The name of "*the LORD*," YHWH (Yah-weh) appears 6,823 times in the inspired Hebrew Scriptures (*The Book of Jewish Knowledge*, p. 184). God said to Moses, "This is my name forever" (Exodus 3:15). God's name as recorded in the Hebrew Scriptures is to remain unchanged throughout all times. To determine the supposedly lost pronunciation of this name we must examine facts that have been accumulated through the centuries by scholars and theologians. These facts can be obtained today by almost anybody, including a child, who is willing to dedicate the time and effort to research more than a single source.

Examine the footnote to Exodus 3:4, in the *Knox* translation of the Bible (Sheed & Ward, Inc.):

> The verb used in the Hebrew text can be translated 'I will be', and it is possible to understand the formula as meaning, 'I will be

what I will be'. In the second half of the verse, according to the Hebrew text, the name used is 'I am' (or, 'I will be'), rather than 'He who is'. But the personal name under which Almighty God was known to the Jews was Yahweh, 'He who is'. The Greek translators, out of reverence, substituted [*Kyrios*] 'the Lord' wherever this name occurred in the Old Testament, and the Latin follows them. Thus, in verse 15 immediately following, 'Yahweh the God of their fathers' appears in the Latin as [*Dominus*] 'the Lord', the God of their fathers'.

Next, look to *The New Oxford Annotated Bible*, and examine the footnote to the same text:

I AM WHO I AM is the etymology of the Israelite name for God: *YHWH*, probably pronounced Yahweh. (The *RSV*, following ancient synagogue practice, substitutes "the Lord"; see the Preface, pp. xi-xii). *YHWH* is treated as a verbal form derived from "to be" and formulated in the first person because God is the speaker. Actually *YHWH* is a third person form and may mean "He causes to be". [*3rd person is a grammatical reference*] …the name was originally pronounced "Yahweh," this pronunciation was not indicated when the Masoretes added vowel signs to the Hebrew text [*about the 8th century A.D.*] (preface to the *RSV*, p. XIV).

In *The Jewish Encyclopedia* (12 vols, Singer, Isador, Phd, ed.) we see that "*YHWH* is the third person singular imperfect 'kal' of the verb *HWH* ('to be') meaning, therefore, 'He is,' or 'He will be,' or, perhaps, 'He lives,' the root idea of the word being, probably, 'to blow,' 'to breathe,' and hence, 'to live.' " (vol. 9: pp. 160-161, "Names of God").

YAHWEH BREATHED HIS NAME INTO MAN

In view of the root of this word, 'to breathe,' consider Genesis 2:7, "And *YHWH* the Mighty One formed man of the dust of the ground, and breathed into his nostrils the breath of life; and man became a living soul." Job said, "The Spirit of God hath made me, and the breath of the Almighty hath given me life." (Job 33:4). YaHWeH is the one who breathes forth life. But he is not just the giver of life, he is also the giver of eternal life. "He who exists eternally," is also "He who causes to exist eternally."

When God breathed life into man's nostrils, he also placed his name in man. With each breath, the divine name proceeds from your mouth, whether you like it or not, and your only escape is in death. The Scripture says, "Let every thing that hath breath praise *YHWH*" (Psalm 150:6) and also, "The dead praise not *YHWH*" (Psalm 115:17).

Listen to yourself breathe. You can detect the name Yahweh, or Yahu, a variant of the same name. Each inhalation produces the effortless pronunciation of the syllable "YA." The exhalation sounds the syllable "HUEH" or "HU." With each complete breath the name of *YaH-WeH* comes forth from the mouth of his creation.

The name also has some connection with a verb "to speak;" Ugaritic: *HWT*, from *HWY*, "word" (*The Interpreter's Dictionary of the Bible*, vol. 2: p. 410). The Creator's name is his Word, which we are now breathing. "Man doth not live by bread only, but by every word that proceedeth out of the mouth of YaHWeH doth man live." (Deuteronomy 8:3; Matthew 4:4). "In the beginning was the Word, and the Word was with God, and the Word was God." This same Word (*YHWH*) created all things, and in him (*YHWH*) was life; and the life was the light of men (John 1:1). Yesu is the Word of God thus Yesu is *YHWH*.

THE LIGHT IS THE LIFE

According to John, Yesu is the light that lights every man that comes into the world. Even the Yogis believe that they are breathing in *prana*, "life force" or "white light," which they say is the Spirit or Breath of God. Often their meditations are in the form of simply listening to one's own breath. Without realizing it they are meditating on the name of the one true God. The living prayer, which is breathed, may be the most perfect form of communication with the Creator; it brings you to the source, for it is the Word of God, *YHWH* Himself.

ERRONEOUS VOWELS ADDED

The name of Yahweh as it appears in the original text is represented by the four Hebrew characters, *yod-he-waw-he* (יהוה) and usually represented by the English "*YHWH*," but sometimes "*IHUH*." According to the *Oxford English Dictionary*, vol. 5: p. 564, "It is now held that the original name was IaHUe(H) ... with the English values of the letters, Yahwe(h)..." In 1530 A.D. the name appeared in Tindale's version of the Bible as Iehouah; in 1539 the Great Bible, Iehoua; 1600 Iehove; 1667 Jehovah; 1738 Jehovah; 1821 Jehovah. "1860 Pusey *Min. Proph. 77*, 'It is better to own ignorance, how this Name of God is pronounced, than to use the name **Jehovah, which is certainly wrong**' ..." (*ibid.*).

The name YHWH has had an interesting history. In the Old Testament period the Hebrew language was written only with consonants; vowels were not added until the Christian era, when Hebrew was no longer a living language. On the basis of Greek texts it is now believed that the original pronunciation of the name was Yahweh. But because of its holy character, the name was withdrawn from ordinary speech during the period after the Exile, and the substitute Hebrew word Adonai, or "Lord," was used (as is still the practice in synagogues). The word **Jehovah** is an artificial form that arose from the **erroneous** combination of the consonants *YHWH* with the vowels of Adonai by a Christian in about the [sixteenth] century A. D. [1518]. In English versions, the name is usually rendered "the Lord." (*Understanding The Old Testament*, p. 34).

How could the name of God have undergone such a change, from Yahweh to Jehovah?

At first Hebrew was written with consonants only, leaving the pronunciation of the vowel sounds to the discretion of the reader. As the language developed certain letters were also used to indicate vowels: *aleph, he* (hay), *waw*, and *yod*. Finally, about the 8th century AD, the Masoretes, Hebrew scribes, devised a system of diacritical points, above, below, and within the consonants, to indicate the proper vowel reading.

The Hebrew Language can be read and understood, by the learned, without the use of written vowels, as witnessed in Modern Hebrew newspapers and many Hebrew books which are printed without the diacritical points.

Some of the antagonists of the Bible Code attempt to discredit the code by convincing the uninformed public that it is illegitimate gibberish because the vowels have been removed from the Hebrew Bible text rendering it illegible. Fact: **No letters have been removed**. Scripture was originally written without vowel points. Fact: Modern Hebrew newspapers are written without vowels. Fact: The Hebrew-speaking people have no problem reading their newspapers and Bibles. Fact: Hebrew written without vowels is just as legible today as it was 3,000+ years ago, when the Torah was first given to Moses directly from heaven.

After the invention of the Masoretic vowel system there have been deceptive points added by the scribes, which if read with the adjoined consonants would produce illegitimate readings. This was done with God's holy name to purposely keep its pronunciation a secret, only for the "chosen" ones.

NAME REMOVED FROM USAGE

The *Shem ha-Meforash*, the "distinctive name," *YHWH* (Yahweh) was considered so sacred that the privilege of learning its pronunciation became reserved to a chosen few, "a small number of esoteric 'elect' of heaven." (*The Book of Jewish Knowledge*, p. 401).

From about 300 BC the name had ceased to be spoken even in Temple worship and as a result the general population had lost its pronunciation. "The sages delivered to their disciples the **KEY** to the Name once every Sabbatical Year [i.e. every seventh year]."

"After the death of the high priest Simeon the Righteous [270 BC] the priests ceased to pronounce the Name (*Yoma* 39b), From that time the pronunciation of the Name was prohibited. 'Whoever pronounces the Name forfeits his portion in the future world' (*Sauh.* xi. 1)." (*The Jewish Encyclopedia*, vol. 9: pp. 162-163).

When Yesu Christ confronted these Doctors of the Law, he said to them, "Woe unto you, Lawyers! for ye have taken away the **KEY** of knowledge [Greek *gnosis*: knowing]: ye entered not in yourselves, and them that were entering in ye hindered." (Luke 11:52). They had taken away the key to knowing the pronunciation of the name. By their failure to use God's name, they excluded themselves from his kingdom, and by forbidding others its use they were actually hindering them from entering the kingdom of Yahweh.

In Malachi 2, Yahweh says to the priests, "If ye will not hear, and if ye will not lay it to heart, to give glory unto my NAME, saith *YHWH* of hosts, I will even send a curse upon you, and I will curse your blessings: yea, I have cursed them already, because ye do not lay it to heart." (v. 2). They had already ceased to use the name of YaHWeH in blessing the people and as a result their blessings became a curse. Yahweh said, "*I will spread dung upon your faces,*" the dung from your sacrifices (v. 3) that is, they will be cast into Gehenna, face-first upon the manure piles to join *Beelzebub,* "the lord of dung." Yahweh will smear their faces with excrement to show what a shameful mess they have become.

The priests were to keep "knowledge," not to cut it off (v. 7). But they departed from the way, causing many to stumble (v. 8).

> After the Exile (6th century B. C.), especially from the 3rd century B.C. on, Jews ceased to use the name Yahweh... As Judaism began to become a universal religion through its proselytizing in the Greco-Roman world, the more common noun *elohim* (q.v.), meaning "god", tended to replace Yahweh. At the same time, the divine name ... was thus replaced in the synagogue ritual by the Hebrew word *Adonai* (My Lord) ...
>
> (*The New Encyclopedia Britannica: Micropedia, Ready Reference*, vol. 10: p.786).

At that time the ancient Illuminati were manipulating the religious hierarchy for their own purpose and plan. These elitists had already hoped to control the world.

RESERVED FOR THE ELITE

Many have conjectured that the reason the ancient Jews forbade the use of the name Yahweh was purely out of reverence, for fear that the name might be taken in vain and profaned by the *goyim* (people, masses, nations, pagans, heathens). But perhaps the reason went much deeper. It may have been a compromise toward the *goyim* whom they wished to win over, for political reasons (Catholicism later accomplished this). To keep from offending pagan ears the name Yahweh was replaced by the more common terms of "Lord" and "God." It may also have been to keep this powerful name of salvation for the elite only, thus eliminating the "chaff" from the Kingdom of God, while at the same time causing them to believe they were part of it.

The religious leaders thought *they* had abolished general use of the name by their own volition, when in truth, God had taken it away from them: "Therefore hear ye the word of

Yahweh, all Judah that dwell in the land of Egypt; Behold, I have sworn by my great name, saith Yahweh, that my name shall no more be named in the mouth of any man of Judah in all the land of Egypt, saying, Lord Yahweh liveth." (Jeremiah 44:26).

In the reading of the Hebrew Scriptures, when the name *YHWH* was encountered, the term *Adonai* (Lord) was pronounced in its place. This practice dated from at least the 3rd century BC. Following after this custom the Masoretes, about the 8th century AD, introduced their vowel points into the Hebrew text and consequently rendered the name *YHWH* with the vowel pointing of the word "*Adonai*" (Heb. *'eDoNaY*) supposedly to assure that the reader would not pronounce the *YHWH* as YaHWeH but would rather insert the word "*Adonai*." This later created a problem for Christian Scribes, unfamiliar with Hebrew practice, yet attempting to translate the Hebrew Scriptures. These vowels from Adonai, e-o-a, written into the name *YHWH*, rendered it as YeHoWaH. With the facts in front of us, we can see that Yehowah is not Yahweh. It is a total misnomer.

Not only did the ancient Jewish hierarchy take away the key of knowledge, but also the Masoretes (Hebrew scholars and scribes) added deceptive vowel signs to the divine name thus causing the ignorant and uninformed to mispronounce it. In the supposed attempt to keep the name from being profaned by the *goyim*, they were actually causing that profanation and blasphemy. Malachi 2, which rebukes the priests for not giving glory to the name *YHWH*, also rebukes the Masoretes and the modern scholars who further perpetrate their fraud: "Judah hath profaned the holiness of *YHWH* ... *YHWH* will cut off the man that doeth this, the master and the scholar ..." (Malachi 2:11-12). Judah (the Jews) had perpetrated the counterfeiting of a false name, which continues to this day, thus profaning the name of Yahweh.

THE SCRIBES WROTE IT WRONG

Although, historically the Israelite scribes copied the Hebrew characters with great accuracy, they later invented and added vowel points which were never a part of the original text and did not exist when it was first written. In some places they purposely inserted false vowels that would result in an erroneous reading for anyone not of the elite.

This was prophesied, "What! *You say, 'We are wise,* we do have his directions' when lo, your scribes have written them wrong and falsified them? No, *the 'wise' shall be discomfited, dismayed and tricked.* They have rejected Yahweh's Word so what wisdom have they?" (Jeremiah 8:8-9, *Moffatt*).

Because of the deceptive vowel points, the name Yahweh became Yehowah. The Latin spelling of this new name was Iehovah (later Jehovah, pronounced Yehowah). "Jehovah' is generally held to be the invention of Pope Leo X's confessor, Peter Galatin ['*De Arcanis Catholisae Veritatis,*' 1518, folio xliii.]." (*The Jewish Encyclopedia*, vol. 7: p. 88).

THE "J" IS A NEW LETTER

Before the 16th century the "J" did not exist in any language of the world. Where did it come from? The J originated as a variant of I, and I is derived from the Greek *iota* and the Semitic *yod*. The I was used as both a vowel and a consonant. Its consonantal sound was that of the English y. Sometime in the early 16th to mid-17th centuries, printers began to prolong the letter I when it appeared as a first or last letter of a word. As an initial letter it extended above and below the line and ended with a curve. As a final form it would extend below the line, used in Latin forms as 'filij', and numerals like j, ij, iij, vj, viij, xij, etc.

Originally, Latin was also without a J. It was "invented by Italian humanists to represent the consonantal i, but now rarely used in classical texts." (Cassell's New Compact Latin-English, English-Latin Dictionary, p.127).

In English it was sometimes used where y had previously been substituted for a final i. It was not until the 17th century that the i was reserved as a vowel and the j as a consonant, and the capital forms of the letter J were introduced (*Oxford English Dictionary*, vol. 5: p. 67).

The differentiation was first made in Spanish, where the capital I had represented both forms, but right around 1600 the capital J began to appear. German printers employed the tailed form of the letter j. Louis Elzevir, who printed at Amsterdam and Leiden 1595-1616, is generally accredited with making the distinction of u/v and i/j, afterwhich in 1619 the capitals U and J were introduced by Lazarus Zetzner of Strasburg. "The Jj types are not used in the Bible of 1611," and "In Dictionaries, the I and J words continued to be intermingled in one series down to the 19th c." (*ibid.*).

The letter J retained the same consonantal "y" sound as its former I. In Anglo-Saxon or Old English there was no J sound. The "dzh" sound of the Modern English J was introduced through the Old French (in modern French the sound is "zh").

It was through the German influence that the w took on the v sound and through the French that the modern English J lost its "y" sound, being replaced by the dzh sound as in jet. Although a few sources believe this may have come about by the 11th century, most references agree that the change did not occur before the late 16th or early 17th century. The name Jehovah is a very recent invention, which, as it is pronounced in the English speaking countries, could not possibly have existed before this time. It could never have appeared in the inspired Scriptures since the Hebrew language did not have a "J" sound (neither did the Greek).

Jehovah: English transliteration of the Divine name, **based on a misunderstanding** of the Hebrew text, which should probably be read Yahweh. (*The Concise Jewish Encyclopedia*, p. 277).

...commonly represented in modern translations by the form "Jehovah", which, however **is a philological impossibility**. (*The Jewish Encyclopedia*, vol. 9: p. 160).

Jehovah: **A mispronunciation** (introduced by Christian theologians, but most entirely disregarded by the Jews) of the Hebrew "*YHWH*," the (ineffable) name of God (the Tetragrammaton or *'Shem ha-Meforash'*). This pronunciation is **grammatically impossible** ... (*ibid.* vol. 7: p. 87).

Jehovah, a **hybrid form** for the divine name which originated in the **mistaken idea** that the consonants of the Tetragrammaton, *YHWH* (really pronounced "Yahweh"), were to be read with the vowel points found with them in the *Masoretic Text*... thus by combining these vowels with the consonants of the Tetragrammaton, the **mongrel form**, "Yehowah," came into being, which with the English consonant j in place of the y and with the German pronunciation of the w as v, produced in turn the quaint form of "Jehovah." (*Encyclopedic Dictionary of the Bible*, p. 1109).

This gross error was definitely made by Christians. The Jews had given up pronouncing the name since the 3rd century BC. It would be better to follow the Jewish tradition in not pronouncing the name at all, rather than to use the falsified name Jehovah. *If we know of this deception* and yet continue to perpetrate the lie, we are ultimately profaning and blaspheming the name of *YHWH*.

PUBLISHING A LIE

Would anyone purposely publish and then knowingly continue to publish this mistake? In answer to this question, see what the Jehovah's Witness' have to say in the forward to the *New World Translation of the Christian Greek Scriptures*:

"While inclining to view the pronunciation 'Yahweh' as the more correct way, we have retained the form 'Jehovah' because of people's familiarity with it ..." (The same quote is found in the preface of *The Kingdom Interlinear Translation of the Greek Scriptures*, 1969).

This is a statement totally contrary to Scriptural principle, for the Apostle Paul said, "...do I now persuade men or God? or do I seek to please men? for if I yet pleased men, I should not be the servant of Christ." (Galatians 1:10).

VAV OR WAW?

In the Sephardic Hebrew, the language of the Scriptures, the *waw* equaled the w sound, i.e. double-u or the oo sound. It did not represent the sound of v, as the Modern Hebrew *vav*. The v sound was accomplished through the letter *beth*, which was otherwise sounded as a letter b. This letter does not appear in the Sacred Name. The Ashkenazi form of Hebrew, less ancient, is read and spoken with Germanic sounds. In this and modern Hebrew, the *waw* has been changed to *vav* and is usually sounded as v. Consequently the Tetragrammaton was never *YHVH* or *JHVH*, but has always been and still is *YHWH*: Yahweh.

> The Modern Hebrew name for this letter [ו] is "vav", a word meaning "peg" or "hook". This letter is used in Modern Hebrew as a consonant with a "v" sound and as a vowel. ...the vowel sound "ow" and ... the vowel sound "uw". When used as a vowel the ancient pronunciation was also an "ow" or "uw". In each of the [four] consonant/vowel letters of the Ancient Hebrew language the pronunciation of the consonant is closely related to the pronunciation of the vowel... For this reason, it is probable that the original pronunciation of the letter [ו] was with a "w". In Modern Arabic language, this letter is also pronounced with a "w". Therefore, the **original name of this letter would have been "waw" instead of "vav".**

("Reconstruction of the Ancient Hebrew Alphabet," *The Ancient Hebrew Research Center, http://www.ancient-hebrew.org/4_alphabet_06.html*).

What is the pronunciation of the name "YHWH" (the LORD)? The Hebrew name for God is a four letter word spelled with four Hebrew letters, yud, hey, vav, hey and transliterated into English as YHVH. ...the Modern Hebrew pronunciation is slightly different than [the] ancient Hebrew pronunciation. ...the letter vav is pronounced with a "v" in modern Hebrew, but was more likely pronounced [in ancient Hebrew] with a "w" hence the often seen transliteration YHWH. ...each of these letters were used as a consonant [as well as] a vowel in Ancient Hebrew. For instance, the letter vav (waw) could be a "W," "O" or "U." ...The two most common pronunciations are Jehovah and Yahweh. Yahweh is a possible translation but not Jehovah as there is no "J" in Hebrew. But, it should be noted that the letter "J" was originally pronounced as a "Y" ... (*ibid. http://www.ancient-hebrew.org/1_faqs.html*).

CORRECT PRONUNCIATION

It is pertinent that we determine the proper pronunciation of the Tetragrammaton, and then use that name, and proclaim it for the glory of God, even if the world, including the religious world, hates us for it. "Ye shall be hated of all men *because of my name*" (Matthew 10:22).

Can we be sure of the correct pronunciation of the Tetragrammaton without the proper diacritical points to determine the vowels? If the four letters of the name are actually vowels, rather than consonants, there is no problem.

TETRAGRAMMATON IN VOWELS

If one ascends to the spiritual world ...one can say that it consists entirely of vowels. ...one enters a tonal world colored in a variety of ways with vowels.... This is why you will find in languages that were closer to the primeval languages that the words for things of the supersensible world were actually vowel-like. The Hebrew word *"Jahve"* for example, did not have the J and the V; it actually consisted only of vowels and was rhythmically half-sung.

(*The Inner Nature of Music and the Experience of Tone*, pp. 37-38)

VOWEL NAME CONFIRMED

Although some authors will make the statement that no letters of the Hebrew alphabet are vowels, any Hebrew grammar will inform you that this is not entirely correct. All of the Hebrew letters are indeed consonants and have a consonantal value, but some of them function additionally as vowels and are so employed. In the past some scholars have condemned the Jewish 1st century historian Josephus for inaccuracies they supposed were to be found in the histories. Nevertheless, recent scholarship has proven Josephus to be accurate in many areas, the Sacred Name being one of them. Scholars had found fault with Josephus because he made the statement that the Sacred Name was four vowels. "A mitre also of fine linen encompassed his head, which was tied by a blue riband, about which there was another golden crown, in which was graven the sacred name [of the Almighty]: it consists of four vowels." This is a description of the headgear worn as the official ceremonial garb by the high priest of Israel. Josephus said that he saw this uniform and he identified the Sacred Name which was engraven into the golden band that held in place the turban (miter) of the high priest. (*YHWH or YHVH?* p. 2).

ALL VOWELS

Treating the Y-H-W-H as vowels (attested to by Josephus) their vocalization would be as follows, *yod* = ee; *he* = ah; *waw* = oo; *he* = eh. As a final letter, *he* in a feminine name would receive an "ah" sound, but in a masculine name it is "eh" or short "e" (*ibid.*). In sounding out these four vowels, ee-ah-oo-eh, the first two, ee-ah, are equivalent to the syllable "Yah"; the last two, oo-eh, equal the sound "weh," as in wet without the t. When pronounced all together, smoothly, the ee-ah-oo-eh becomes Yahweh.

The beauty in this *all-vowel* name is that it flows with the breath. When a vowel is articulated there is no obstruction in the throat or mouth. The sound flows smoothly and without hindrance all the way from the diaphragm. Because the name consists of pure vowels it flows effortlessly with the breath as a spontaneous action.

When you say Yahweh, ee-ah-oo-eh, the lips and throat never close. The tongue never touches the teeth or the roof of the mouth. If a person had their tongue cut out they could still say the name of Yahweh. Even without lips or teeth the pronunciation would not be impeded. It is essentially a sound that floats on the breath.

The Greek *all-vowel* transliteration of the divine name is *Iaoue*. It is sounded out exactly the same as in Hebrew. The *I* = ee; *a* = ah; *ou* = oo; *e* = eh: *ee-ah-oo-eh*, Yahweh.

The languages of the Bible, Hebrew/Aramaic and Greek, are the witnesses that the true pronunciation of the heavenly Father's name is Yahweh. Since neither the Hebrew nor the

Greek had a J or a J-sound, it is impossible for the sacred name ever to have been Jehovah or Jahveh.

When you see the Tetragrammaton, the Hebrew vowel-letters יהוה, *YHWH*, or in the *King James Version* Bible "the LORD," with LORD in capitals, you should read Yahweh.

It is not just a matter of semantics. There are definitely some very serious problems and concerns with the name Jehovah, especially since God said his name is Yahweh and warned that anyone changing even one of his words would be cursed to destruction and death (see, Revelations 22:18-19; cf. Deuteronomy 4:2-3). Directly after posing the question, "What is his name and what is the name of his son," a warning is issued not to change his word, or you will be reproved as a liar (Proverbs 30:4-6).

THERE WAS NO JESUS EITHER

Since there is no J in the Greek or Hebrew languages, in which the Bible was written, what of the name Jesus?

There was no Jesus before the 17th century. The name Jesus did not exist in any language in the world; not even English.

"During the Middle English period [the name of the Saviour was] regularly used in its Old French (objective) form *Iesu*. The (Latin nominative) form *Iesus* was rare in Middle English, but became the regular English form in 16th century. Yet in *Tindale's New Testament*, 1525-34, the form Iesu was generally used where the Greek had *Iesou*, the Vulgate *Iesu*... This was, as a rule, retained by *Coverdale* 1535, and in the *Great Bible* 1539..." (*The Oxford English Dictionary* [in 12 vols.] vol. 5: p. 573).

The name appears in English Bibles and Historical works, as Iesu (pronounced yay-soo), prior to 1633 AD, afterwhich, it begins to appear as Jesu. Finally in the year 1779 we find the spelling Jesus being commonly used, but not exclusively, for Jesu is still used through 1827 and probably as late as 1881. (For a detailed etymology please consult the previously cited reference book). The *Jesus* spelling may have come into existence as early as

1775, or 1776, along with the Satanic declaration "Don't Tread on Me." According to Benjamin H. Freedman there was no word "Jew" before this time either. "It is an incontestable fact that the word 'Jew' did not come into existence until the year 1775. Prior to 1775 the word 'Jew' did not exist in any language." (*Facts are Facts*, p. 12). We did not have a letter J.

NAME PROGRESSION CHART

> # Progression in the English Translation from
> # Iesu (Yesu = yay-soo) to Jesus

1175	Iesu		1611	Iesu, Iesus
1240	Iesu		1633	Jesu
1377	Iesu, Ihesu		1641	Iesu
1435	Iesu		1676	Jesu
1526	Iesu, Ihesus		1740	Jesu
1534	Iesu, Iesus		1779	Jesus
1544	Ihesus		1827	Jesu
1552	Iesu		1881	Jesus

This chart was compiled according to the etymological information given in volume six, page 573, of the *Oxford English Dictionary in Twelve Volumes*. According to this and other information the *King James Version* of 1611 contained the name of Yesu (Iesus). This is witnessed in a 1611 reproduction (Thomas Nelson Publishers). The Jesu forms were also pronounced Yesu, as in German (J=Y). Time has hardened the J and softened the e, and along with the inflectional s, the fraudulent name of Jesus was born. Jesu first appeared from 1633 to 1740, with a return to the Iesu in 1641. This shows that it was still being used. By 1779 Jesus appeared. Jesu resurfaced in 1827, but after 1881 Jesus prevails. Some researchers feel that Jesus may have come into usage by 1776, about the same time as the Satanic statement, "Don't Tread On Me."

THERE WAS NO "J"

Anyone can look into an unabridged dictionary and ascertain that since there was no J before the late 16th or early 17th century, the Saviour's name could not possibly be Jesus (gee-zus).

The development of the pronunciation of the name has been altered from Yay-soo (with inflection, Yay-sooce) to Jay-sooce and finally to Jee-zus which is the modern English pronunciation.

CORRECT PRONUNCIATION IMPERATIVE

In the late 1970's, I became concerned about the true pronunciation of the Saviour's name. At that time I received information from K. M. Bean, an Ohio Bible scholar and student of the Biblical languages, stating that the Saviour's name in Ancient Hebrew is pronounced Yay-soo, the same as in the *Koine* (common) Greek. I began to do a follow-up. Before getting very far, there were others assuring me that it did not matter. They attempted to convince me that names change from one language to another, but as we have seen, the Saviour's name did not change when translated into English; it was changed many years later.

Until 1980, I thought little more about it. When I presented these findings to Dr. Oliver Blosser, PhD, an eminent Greek and Hebrew scholar with whom I had often consulted, he confirmed the information was correct, as to the pronunciation, but that in his opinion it did not matter, since Jesus is (supposed to be) the English equivalent of that name.

In January of 1982, I was stirred into deeper study by the Holy Spirit. Sometime in February, that year, I became thoroughly convinced that the correct pronunciation of the Saviour's name is imperative. After an additional 300 hours of intense research there was no doubt his name in Old English and Early Modern English, was pronounced yay-soo, exactly the same as it had been in the Biblical languages. Many languages of the world still have the correct pronunciation today. The best Modern English transcription is Yesu.

YESU'S NAME IN THE WORLD TODAY

Yesu(s) name is Pronounced in many Languages:

The Welsh, Hawaiian, Latin, Samoan, New Hebridian, and many other languages use IESU (some use Yesu or Isus) as LORD's name today. Chinese Mandarin, Cantonese, Chibemba, Bambara, Bukusu, Indonesian, Luba Kaonde, Malay, Afrikaans, Greek, Korean, Thai, Javanese, Kamba, Kiluba, Kinandi, Tsonga, Changana, Kinyarwanda, Luganda, Lugbara, Luo, Tyap, Tiv, Runyoro, Runyankole/Rukiga, Swahili, Zaire Swahili, German, Standard Arabic, Hindi... Japanese and many other languages pronounce LORD's name as [yesu] or [yesus]! Some pronounce [yesou], [yeso], [yasu], or [yasou].

It is okay to change Iohn, Ioseph, Iames, and Iob to John, Joseph, James, and Job respectively; but it is not okay to change Iesu to Jesus! Because the holy name IESU is not an ordinary name! "Holy Father, protect them by the power of your name — *the name you gave me* — so that they may be one as we are one." (John 17:11b) By the power of the holy name of the LORD GOD, we need to restore the unity of Christians ("the church's present divisions are the result of the failures of Christians," quoted from *The New Study Bible, New International Version*, Zondervan Bible Publishers, 1985, p.1630.) To restore the unity of Christians, we need first to reach the unity of the western language spelling and pronunciation of the name of the LORD GOD – IESU.

The name "IESU" has been used in the Bible for more than 1900 years; "IESU" & "IESUS" was changed to "JESUS" in 17th century. "IESU" is the holy name of the LORD GOD. Check how many times "the LORD" and "GOD" were used together in the New Testament, especially in the Book of Revelation (Revelation 1:7-8; 4:8; 4:11; 11:17; 15:3; 16:7; 18:8; 19:6; 21:22; 22:5; Matthew 4:7; 4:10; 22:37; Mark 12:29; 12:30; Luke 1:6; 1:16; 1:32; 1:47; 1:68; John 20:28; Acts 2:39; 3:22; 4:24; Jude:24,25.)

(http://home.comcast.net/~yjt712/LORD-IESU).

BIBLICAL ETYMOLOGY OF THE NAME YESU

The Hebrew language was the original language of Israel and of the Holy Scripture [O.T.]. The first form of Christ's name is found in the book of Numbers. Moses had a helper named HWS` (Nu. 13:8,16). Moses renamed HWS` (Helper) by adding the first letter of God's name, it then read: YHWS` (which presumably meant, YHWH is the helper). The word YHWS` was changed to (YSW`) in the days of Ezra and Nehemiah. This final form (YSW`) was transliterated by Jewish scholars in the Septuagint Scripture (Greek) in the 3rd century B.C. as [*Iesou*: e.a.sou] (which sounded exactly like the Hebrew name).

The actual pronunciation of the Hebrew ...must depend upon the Greek, since this was the first language with vowels into which the Hebrew Scripture was translated [1,000 yrs. before the Masoretes introduced their vowel signs].

The transliteration (bringing over the sound from one language into another) of the Greek word into English is Yasu [yay-soo].... Since the Greek name of Christ was pronounced Yasu, and the Greek sounded exactly like the Hebrew, YSW` also was pronounced Yasu [yay-soo].

Greek was the world-wide language at the time of Christ and His apostles. The good news of Christ therefore was first spread in the Greek language....

Since God chose this Holy name, Yasu, by which to save his people [Matt. 1:21; Lk. 24:47; Acts 10:43; etc.] it evidently is of utmost importance, and should not be changed. God ordained that His saving name should be pronounced Yasu [yay-soo]. Who is man to say that God's name is not important enough to keep its original pronunciation and should now follow the false church's practice of calling His name "Jesus"? (*Who Is God?* K.M. Bean).

Moses' helper Joshua (*Yehowshuwa/Yesu*) is an Old Testament typology of Christ the Saviour and a potential record of the etymology of the Saviour's name, Yesu. The verb from which this name is formed is *YS`*, meaning *safety, help, protection,* thus the name *HWS`* (Hosea) meaning *deliverer* or *helper*. As we have already seen, Hebrew was at first written with only consonants. Before the vowel points were added certain letters had come also to indicate vowels, "This is still inconsistent in the spelling of the Hebrew Bible ... the same form or word being written sometimes with [vowel letters], sometimes without" (*The New Standard Jewish Encyclopedia*, p. 1928). In Numbers 13:16, Moses changed the name of HWS` by adding the first letter of the Tetragrammaton, *yod*, making it YHWS`. This name is also found written in Deuteronomy 3:21, as YHWSW`. The second W represents a vowel U = oo. With or without the second *waw*, it is the same name: early form Yahoshu(a) or Yahosu(a), later form Yesu, represented in the LXX (Greek *Septuagint*) by *Iesou*, but in Modern English Bibles by "Joshua" or "Jesus." The name means "Yahweh helper" or "Help of Yahweh," also translated "Salvation (or Help) is of Yahweh," i.e. "Yahweh (is helper)

Saviour." Psalm 124:6 says, "Our help is in the name of *YHWH*," and Hebrews 13:6, "The Lord (*YHWH*) is my helper."

The name of the same man, YHWS`, appears in Nehemiah 8:17, written as ישוע, YSW`: Yesu`, i.e. Yesu (yay-soo).

The name of God, *YHWH* (Yahweh) is signified in proper names by YHW, at the beginning or end, also by YH (*yod, he*) at the end, or simply by *yod* in the beginning. The YSW` spelling of the name signifies that *Yahweh is the Saviour*.

The first syllable of this name represents YHWH. The second syllable, originally HWS`, simply meant helper or deliverer, but in its latter form, SW`, it takes on an even deeper significance. First of all it is used in the sense of *to be free or safe*, as a causative and reflexive to halloo, i.e. *to be saved or set free* in answer to one's cry for help. It also gives the implication of being *rich*. Secondly, it means *to halloo*, "to pursue with shouts; shout with a loud voice." What did Joshua do at Jericho?

Read Joshua 6:1-20. He and the people shouted with a great shout and the walls of the city fell and the people ascended up on the seventh day, a typology of Yahweh's salvation. According to 1Thessalonians 4:16-17, "Yahweh himself shall descend from heaven with a shout ..." which will raise the dead so that both they and the living saints, which have been chosen as the Bride of Christ, will be caught up together to meet him In the air.

The name Yesu, the late form of Joshua *(Yehoshua)*, more fully means, "Yahweh is the Saviour who answers your cry and will call you up," i.e. "come up hither." The call to the Bride is a two-way call. He will call those up who have called upon Him.

Under the name Jesus, the *Etymological Dictionary of the English Language* by Rev. Walter W. Skeat, has, "the Saviour of mankind. (L.-Gk.-Heb.) In Wyclif's Bible. -- L. *Iesus* (Vulgate). -- G. *Iesous*. -- Heb. *Yeshu`a* (Jeshua, Nehemiah viii. 17, a later form of Joshua): contracted form of *Yehoshu`a* (Jehoshua, Numbers 13:16), signifying, '[Yahweh] is salvation' or 'Saviour.' " (p. 314).

John L. McKenzie, in his *Dictionary of the Bible*, says, "Jesus Christ. 1. *Name.* Greek *iesous* represents Hebrew and Aramaic *yesu`a....* The meaning of the name ("Yahweh is salvation") ... Matthew 1:21; Luke 2:21 ..." (p. 432).

YESHUA IS IMPROPER

The correct name and proper pronunciation of names is important. Someone by the name Robert may answer to Bob, but a person surnamed Bob would not respond to the name Robert because that is not his name. Yeshua may be related to Yesu, but Yesu is the Biblically recorded name that has been the appellation of Christ since the beginning of time, and Yesu is not necessarily synonymous with Yeshua.

Many Christian scholars believe that the name of Christ in Hebrew was *Yeshua*. But the name which is pronounced Yeshua (yeh-shoo-ah, or, y'shua) by Modern Christian scholars is not pronounced that way by the Jews (with few exceptions) in reference to Christ. The final letter, *ayin* (eye-in) represented by ` is not heard in the pronunciation (*Dictionary of the Bible*, p. 71, McKenzie). The *ayin* is usually neglected, although it appears in writing (cf. *Beginners' Hebrew Grammar*, Rev. Harold L. Creager, B.D., p. 6). An *ayin* at the end of a word does not inevitably change its pronunciation, neither would an *alef* or *he*. Modern Hebrew dictionaries do not even print the *ayin* in the name Yesu, but simply print the three letter spelling, *yod*, *shin*, *waw*.

In his Bible Code book, Scholar and researcher, Jeffrey Satinover, states, "The silent letters in Hebrew are '*aleph*' and '*ayin*', which can take on any vowel sound. Many words are spelled with them or without them." (*Cracking The Bible Code*, p. 312). The "a" vowel of the final syllable in Yeshua is not derived from the *ayin*, but from the deceptive Masoretic points which did not appear before the 8th century AD. "One has to be careful not to grant the same canonical authority to the Masoretes as to Moses and the prophets. Nor should one be too critical of the modern Old Testament scholar who thinks he has just cause to alter one or two of the signs the Masoretes had introduced." (*Do It Yourself Hebrew and Greek: Everybody's Guide to the Language Tools, p.* 14:3).

If the *ayin* had been pronounced it could have represented either of two sounds, *g* or *h*, according to various Hebrew Grammars and *Septuagint* study. But in the name which we are scrutinizing, we can be relatively certain that it was ignored or practically silent, because it was not transliterated in the *Septuagint*.

A *g*-sound would have called for a Greek rendering of *Iesoug*, which is not the case. An *h*-sound, preceded by a vowel, would scarcely be heard and need not appear in transliteration at all.

"*Ayin* is an aspiration midway in strength between *alef* and *he*. We transliterate it by a rough breathing ['], and practically neglect it in pronunciation." (*Beginners' Hebrew Grammar*, p. 6). Yesu and Yesuh would be identical in pronunciation. A word can be closed with an unsounded consonant. The "moveable" *ayin* (even when not pronounced, *ayin* is categorized as a *moveable* letter) can be used in closing, the same as a "silent" *alef* or *he*.

In the Talmudic spelling of the same name, the *ayin* has actually disappeared. Rather than YSW` (*yod, shin, waw, ayin*) the name is simply YSW (ישׁי, *yod, shin, waw*). This confirms that the two spellings are the same one identical name, and "Yesu" is the pronunciation. The Talmud refers to him as YSW HNOTSRY (*Yesu ha Notsriy*: Yesu the Nazarene; *Notsriy* also means Christian).

> The name "Jesus" is an ENGLISH, not an APOSTOLIC name! …the Hebrew name "Yeshua" is not the name of the Messiah. Although this name for the Messiah is Hebrew, it is modern Hebrew. This is not the Paleo-Hebraic form (ancient Hebrew). …
>
> …In Aramaic, Jesus' name would have been **pronounced *Yesu* by the Galileans**, and as *Yeshu* in southern Israel, because they were typically able to pronounce the "sh" sound of the Hebrew letter *shin*, whereas northern Israelites could not (See Judges 12:5-6).
>
> (*http://www.apostolic.net/biblicalstudies/yeshua.htm*).

Like the California group, *Jews for Jesus*, Grant Jeffrey and Yacov Rambsel, in their Bible Code books, use the name Yeshua synonymously with Jesus. Grant Jeffrey says Yeshua is "Jesus," and promotes the name Yeshua over the name Yeshu (Yesu) which he insinuates is incorrect. What he does not realize is that the Hebrew/Aramaic three-letter and four-letter spellings of the Saviour's name are pronounced the same, Yesu or Yeshu, not Yeshua. **The Bible Code programs all have the three-letter spelling**, not the four, in their data bases. **All the Hebrew dictionaries have the three-letter spelling** also, and not the four-letter spelling.

YSW CANNOT BE OBLITERATED

Mr. Jeffrey suggests the name of Yeshu (Yesu) comes from a derogatory acronym, *Yimach Shemo Uzikhro* [or, *yemach shemo vezichro*] "May his name and memory be blotted out" (*The Mysterious Bible Codes*, pp. 99-100). The initial letters of these three words, the *Yod Shin Waw* (YSW) do spell the name of Yesu. The curse is actually pronounced with the words *Yemach shemo*, "his name shall be erased." According to *Ben Yehuda's English-Hebrew/Hebrew-English Pocket Dictionary* (p. xxiii) the abbreviation for the *yemach shemo vezichro* curse is YMS, *Yod Mem Shin*, for *Yemach shemo*, and not YSW. If a person's name were to be blotted out and remembered no more, it would have to never be written again, otherwise the purpose would be defeated. It would perpetuate that name rather than destroy it. If the YSW acronym were used as an abbreviation for the curse, every time it was written down it would proclaim the name of Yesu. Rather than blot out his name it would actually preserve it.

His name cannot be obliterated. In fact, every time the curse would be pronounced upon someone, their name would be obliterated while simultaneously being overwritten by the name of Yesu (YSW). In a sense, this happens to us. We are cursed because of sin. When we repent and are baptized, Yesu's name is called out over us. We are superimposed by his name and he has become the "curse" for us (Galatians 3:13). "Cursed is everyone that hangeth on a tree" (Deuteronomy 21: 22-23). It is only appropriate that the letters of his name, ישׁו (YSW) would stand as an acronym for the curse.

These letters (ישׁו) also spell, "his existence." Reversed, they spell, "and gift." The primary meaning of the name Yesu is, "Yahweh the Saviour." The symmetrical analysis of the name, when it is read forward and then backward, says, "His existence, and Gift."

AUTHORITIES CONFIRM YESU/YESHU

Many Christian Hebrew scholars, refer to Christ as Yeshua or Y'shua, while Jewish Hebrew scholars confirm that the name is pronounced Yeshu, or Yesu. Rabbi Robert Schectman, Cnesses Israel Congregation, Green Bay, Wisconsin, states, "This name is used only in reference to Christ, and it is never pronounced Yeshua." (c. 1982). Whether the three-letter spelling is used or the four, with the ayin, it is still not pronounced Yeshua. He said, although this pronunciation may be a possibility it is not used. "The pronunciation in Aramaic was probably Yeshu, or Yesu." Aramaic was the language used by the Jews of that period and referred to in the Bible as Hebrew. These echoed the words of his predecessor Rabbi Vande Walle.

Other members of the Jewish community, Cnesses Israel, verified, "The name of *Jesus* in Hebrew is pronounced Yesu." According to most Jews, the Hebrew name of Christ is Yesu (pronounced Yay-soo) although some may pronounce it Yeshu. The English transliteration from the Talmud is "Yeshu." The e is pronounced like the e in they, as a long *a*-sound.

While filming an apocalyptic art documentary in Douglas, Arizona with the Disinformation Company in 1999, the cameraman, an Israelite, had just come to the States. He grew up in Israel and speaks the Hebrew language fluently. Asked about the pronunciation of the name in Israel, he said Yesu, or Yeshu is the only name used to refer to Christ, and that Yeshua is never used.

TWO DIALECTS

Vande Walle and Schectman indicated that there were two different dialects among the tribes of Israel. In the spelling of a given word, one would pronounce the *sin* (seen), the other, *shin* (sheen). The *s* or *sh*-sound was irrelevant in pronunciation, since words spelled with *sin* or *shin* were sometimes interchanged by the letter *camek* (*c* = *s*). Shectman explained that, in view of the two dialects, either pronunciation would be correct, Yeshu or Yesu. It is certain the name being referred to was not pronounced Yeshua or Yahshua, and could never be pronounced Jesus (gee-zus).

The Masoretes pointed the letter *sin* making it *shin* or the "*sh*" in Yeshu. In pointed script *sin* has a dot over its left shank, *shin* has one over its right, "undistinguishable in unpointed script." (*The Book of Jewish Knowledge*, p. 1758). "Probably the sounds were not differentiated in the early language" (*Beginners' Hebrew Grammar*, p. 5).

"The changes undergone by Hebrew pronunciation are ...obscured, but they can to some extent be traced through transliterations of words into Assyrian (9th-6th centuries B.C.), Greek (4th century B.C. - 4th century A.D.)... In Europe, *sh* and *s* were confused until 1100 [A.D.]." (*The New Standard Jewish Encyclopedia*, p. 872). To trace the exact pronunciation of YSW`, it will then be necessary to look to the Greek transliteration:

"*Iesous* is the Greek form of the Old Testament Jewish name *Yesua*`, arrived at by transcribing the Hebrew and adding an -s to the nominative to facilitate declension. Yesua` (Joshua) seems to have come into general use about the time of the Babylonian exile in place of the older Yehosua`. The LXX [Greek translation of O.T.] rendered both the ancient and more recent forms of the name uniformly as *Iesous*." (*The New International Dictionary of the New Testament Theology*, vol. 2: pp. 330-331).

Greek as well as Hebrew is an inflectional language. Inflection is "the variation or change of form which words undergo to mark distinctions of case, gender, number, tense, person, mood, voice, etc." The Saviour's name, in the Greek, may be found written *Iesou*, *Iesous* or *Iesoun* depending upon how it is used in the sentence. The root is *Iesou*, the same as the Hebrew *YSW*, Yesu.

The I is the Greek *Iota* (ee-oh-tah = yota) and is vocalized as "*ee*". When it precedes another vowel it sounds like y. The second letter in the name is the Greek *Eta* (ay-tah) long *e* as in *they*. This first part of the name is then vocalized as *ee-ay*, which is equal to the syllable yay. The letters which follow, *Sigma*, *Omicron*, *Upsilon*, are sounded as *soo*. Therefore, the entire name is pronounced yay-soo. In Greek, when the name is used as the subject of a sentence (nominative) it ends in s. As a direct object (vocative) it ends in n. In all other cases, the base, *Iesou* is used. The s and n are merely inflections. The name is not *Iesous* anymore than it is *Iesoun*, but rather these are inflectional forms of the same unchanged name: *Iesou*, Yesu.

The Hebrew YSW` means "He shall save, deliver... Hence, Gr. *Iesou*, A Saviour, from *sao* or *sou*, to save, deliver, heal, restore." (*A Complete Hebrew and English Critical and Pronouncing Dictionary*, p. 329). In Greek an s was added to the nominative form but when the name is translated into non-inflectional languages the s is dropped. English is a non-inflectional language. The early English translators were correct in dropping the s and also the n. from the Messiah's name. Their transliteration was Iesu.

According to grammatical rules, "In transcribing Greek words into English: Transliterate the Greek word into Latin first and then into English." (*Greek and Latin in Scientific Terminology*, p. 56). "In general there is a tendency to drop the inflectional endings since in English they rarely serve, as they do in Latin and Greek, to indicate the grammatical function of the word in a sentence." (*ibid*. p. 44). In the English language an s added to the end of a word serves to alter it from singular to plural (e.g. horse, horses; cow, cows) or to show possession.

Since we are working from the nominative Greek form *Iesous*, first transliterate to the Latin nominative, *Iesus*, then drop the inflection to arrive at the English transcription, Iesu. Remember, in English to add an s to this base would form a plural. Due to changes in our language, the best Modern English representation is Yesu (Yasu has been used also).

Instead of following the established rules of transliteration, the modern translators have followed the trend of the language, using a J instead of an I or Y. They also returned the inflectional s, so the name became Jesus. With other Biblical names the inflection is dropped in the transliteration from Greek to English. For example: *Paulos* becomes Paul; *Markos* is Mark; *Stephanos* is Stephen; *Timotheos* is Timothy, etc. Even *Christos* becomes "Christ" in English, yet the modern translators fail to drop the inflection from the Saviour's name.

The early Christians, whether Jew or Gentile, even the Early American Christians, called the Saviour Yesu. Modern Christians should do the same.

> Talmudic Judaism... accustomed itself, when it was obliged to name Jesus of Nazareth, to referring to him as Yesu and not as Yesua`. **Christians referred to their Lord as Yesu** (formed from the divine name and *sua*, from the root *ys`*) which, as we have shown, has a continuing life in the Greek *Iesous*: "Yahweh is our help" or "Yahweh is our helper"... (*The New International Dictionary of New Testament Theology*, vol. 2: pp. 330-332).

In the Tulmud, *Sanhedrin* 432-436, we find that the name is mentioned in the English translation not as *Jesus* but rather "*Yeshu*" the Nazarene. Another Jewish reference calling him Yeshu is that of the *Toledot Yeshu* (Hebrew: "*History of [the Life of] Yesu*") which is a medieval pseudo-history of the life of Yesu. These sources clearly show that the Aramaic name was not pronounced Yeshua (Yay-shoo-a), as it usually is today by the modern Christian student of Hebrew, but that there was no final syllabic "a". Biblical and historical information is sufficient to determine that the name, in reference to Christ, is Yesu.

YESU PRESERVED IN GREEK

In unpointed script it would be difficult to trace the exact pronunciation at this late date. Transliterations from the Hebrew into Koine Greek have helped to preserve the correct pronunciation.

By the time of the Christian era, Greek was the predominant language of the entire known world. When Alexander conquered the Persian Empire, in 333 BC, his conquest extended the spread of Greek culture which had begun in the Near East in the 7th century BC.

> As a result of his conquest the Greek Language was spread among all nations and became the common medium of communication... Not only the Jews of the dispersion but those who remained in the land gradually took up the Greek Language. Hence, when the Scriptures were translated into that tongue, the Hebrew text was soon left for the rabbis in the synagogues. The Greek translation took its place in common use. While some still retained a small smattering of the language of inspiration, the tongue of the Jews became Greek. Our Lord and his disciples spoke Greek. Only occasionally they used a familiar word or phrase from the Aramaic, which was probably a corruption of the ancient Hebrew. ...the Jews themselves could be reached only by the use of Greek. ...

> Doubtless it was God's plan to use this change in language to reach the other nations ... But the use of Greek was quite as necessary to reach the Jews themselves both in the land and among the dispersion. (*The Concordant Version of the Sacred Scriptures*, p.37, introduction).

In the last quarter of the fourth century B.C., Alexandria rose in Egypt as a cultural center and continued as the intellectual center of the world during the third and second centuries. The many Jews there — some had migrated from Palestine while others had moved up from other parts of Egypt — began to speak Greek to such an extent that they even forgot Aramaic. (By this time Hebrew was used only for scholarly and liturgical purposes.) This necessitated a Greek translation of the Jewish Scriptures, which was undertaken in Alexandria. The Greek Old Testament is known as the *Septuagint*. (*"A Survey of Biblical Geography,"* p. 39: *The New American Bible*.)

The Greek Old Testament is called the *Septuagint* (Seventy) because it is believed to have been translated by seventy men. It is sometimes represented by the Roman numerals LXX. The LXX translation was accomplished in the 3rd century BC (around 280).

At the time of Christ, Greek was a very widely spoken language in the Roman Empire. It was the national language, more so than Latin. People of all nationalities spoke Greek. The fact that Greek had become such a universal language was a great help in the spread of the gospel of Christ. The Apostles were able to teach from the Greek Septuagint Scriptures and to spread the word of God in a language which the people of all lands understood. They were also able to write their instructions to the churches in the language of the land. Thus, the Greek New Testament was born.

The name *Iesou* appears in the Greek New Testament. The Greek Old Testament transliterates the Saviour's name from the Hebrew YSW` by rendering it also as *Iesou*.

In the study of Greek words which have been transliterated from the Hebrew, it appears that words having a simple s sound are transliterated by a single s, while Hebrew words with the sh sound are usually represented by a double sigma (ss), e.g. "Jesse" (Heb. *Yishay*, Gr. *Iessai*) and "Messiah" (Heb. *Mashiyach*, Gr. *Messias*). The Greek language had no sh sound. They seem to have indicated the sh sound with the double s, like in English where *mission* is pronounced "mish-un," *session* is "sesh-un," and issue is "ish-you". This principle seems to follow through, so if the Messiah's name had been Yeshu, the Greek transliteration should have been Iessou, in keeping with the cited Hebrew to Greek transliterations. Since the Greek is Iesou we have no reason to suspect anything other than the straight s-sound. It accurately represents the Hebrew YSW` and is correctly pronounced **Yesu (yay-soo) exactly as the Galileans pronounced it** (re. p.152).

YESU PRESERVED IN LATIN

The Latin language is another witness to the Saviour's name. When Christ was crucified a nameplate was affixed to the head of his cross. The plate was entitled in three languages, "Hebrew, and Greek, and Latin." (John 19:19-20). No one thought there were three different names on this plaque. There was one name written in three languages. The Hebrew YSW` and the Greek *Iesou* (with inflection: *Iesous*) appeared in Latin form as *IESVS* (base: *IESV= Iesu*). When those passing by read the inscription, whether they read the Hebrew, Greek, or Latin, the name they read was Yesu. They pronounced it yay-soo. No one thought there were three people hanging on one cross, and no one thought there were three different names on the inscription plate. The Greek and Latin are *two testimonies* of the one true pronunciation of the Hebrew or Aramaic YSW`.

Practically every available reference tells us that Jesus is the Latin form of the Greek *Iesou(s)* and Hebrew YSW`. A glance into any Latin grammar or dictionary will show that the proper pronunciation of *Jesus* is Yay-sooce. By correctly dropping the inflection, when transcribing into English, you will see that the name is Yesu. The traditional English pronunciation of Jesus (gee-zus) is a mispronunciation of the Latin transcription. It is this J-E-S-U-S spelling which has caused so much confusion in pronunciation from one language to another.

NATIONAL LANGUAGE

At the time in which the Messiah first appeared there was a national language in which the gospel could be easily communicated. God could have chosen any language he pleased for a national language. He chose for it to be Greek. He would not have chosen Greek if his saving name could not be communicated in that language.

Some scholars erroneously say that we cannot trust the Greek Scriptures for the pronunciation of Messiah's name and that the Greek New Testament is uninspired. They say the inspired New Testament was written in Hebrew. Yet there are over 4,600 Greek manuscripts in existence (*Aid to Bible Understanding*, p. 1108) and not even a portion of one authentic original Hebrew New Testament.

The Old Testament was originally written in Hebrew and Aramaic (a Hebrew dialect) and had to be translated into Greek so people could read it. It would not have been feasible to write the New Testament in Hebrew, that would then have to be translated into Greek which was the national language of the empire.

TAKEN AWAY THE KEY

Would the Creator leave us without an accurate record of his name? Greek is our basic key to the name as it appears in the unpointed Hebrew. We are not looking for a sacred language but rather the pronunciation of a sacred name. Yahweh chose the Greek language as the key to pronouncing his name as God and Saviour, let us not be guilty of taking away that key like the Modern English translators have done. They are in the same category with the scribes of old: *they have taken away the key of knowledge.* Our forefathers knew the true name because "In early modern English Bibles Iesu [Yesu] was the distinctive form for the oblique cases [Latin *obliquis*; *ob*, before, and *liquis*, away, turned, or twisted.]; it was frequent in the earlier forms of the *Book of Common Prayer*." (*The Oxford Dictionary of English Etymology*, p. 494).

The true pronunciation of Yesu is retained in the African and Oriental Languages even today. Although English-speaking missionaries are perpetually attempting to change it.

Brother K. W. Kraus shares a house in Dallas, Texas, with an African man who speaks ten languages. Seven of those languages are Ugandan dialects. He confirms that Yesu is the pronunciation in all seven dialects. He also states that all Africans, from all African countries, pronounce the Saviour's name Yesu (yay-soo) not Jesus. He also noted that they never use the false name Jehovah, but pronounce God's holy name Yahweh.

The German language retains a pronunciation close to the original. In German the name is spelled Jesu and pronounced Yay-zoo. Whenever you are reading and you come across the name Jesus, remember, the English language has developed from the inflectional to the analytical type of speech. **The final s is inflectional and should be dropped**, leaving Jesu, which should be pronounced with a near German pronunciation, but giving a sharp s rather than a z sound, so that when you are seeing Jesus you are reading and pronouncing "Yesu" (Yay-soo).

YAHSHUA IS ERRONEOUS

The Sacred Name proponents claim that the Messiah's name is Yahshua and this is why they deny the authenticity of the Greek Scriptures, stating that the Saviour's name is Hebrew. Yet, even the Hebrew translations of the Greek New Testament present the name as Yesu (YSW`) and not Yahshua (photostatic reproduction appears in the forward of *The Kingdom Interlinear Translation of the Greek Scriptures*, p. 21).

> "Yahshua" is a mistransliteration by Sacred Name advocates to fit an erroneous interpretation of John 5:43... (Dr. Daniel Botkin)
>
> Dr. Danny Ben-Gigi says of the Yahshua form that "there is no such name in Hebrew" and that

"people invented it to fit their theology." Dr. Ben-Gigi is an Israeli and the former head of Hebrew programs at Arizona State University. He is the author of the book First Steps in Hebrew Prayers, and he designed and produced the "Living Israeli Hebrew" language-learning course.

Dr. David Bivin, a Christian, says that the Yahshua form "is rooted in a misunderstanding." Dr. Bivin is a renowned Hebrew scholar and teacher and author of Fluent Biblical Hebrew....

To people who actually know Hebrew — people like Dr. Ben-Gigi, Dr. Bivin, and others — it is very obvious that those who insist on the Yahshua form know very little about the Hebrew language....

"John Briggs and Paul Penn were the FIRST to pronounce and use the name Yahshua" (emphasis Snow's). This was in 1936 and in 1937, the article states. No information is given about how Briggs and Penn came up with this (mis)translation.

(http://www.yashanet.com/library/Yeshua_or_Yahshua. htm).

YESU IS SCRIPTURAL

Yesu Christ said, "Search the Scriptures; for in them ye think ye have eternal life: and they are they which testify of me." (John 5:39). The Apostle Paul said to Timothy, "from a child thou hast known the Holy Scriptures which are able to make thee wise unto salvation through faith which is in Christ *Iesou* [Yesu]." (2Timothy 3:15). The Scriptures of which the Messiah and Paul were speaking are the Old Testament Scriptures. The New Testament did not yet exist. The Old Testament Scriptures do not testify of Jesus or Yahshua, but of Yesu, and are able to give you knowledge unto salvation through faith which is in Christ Yesu.

In the Old Testament the name of Yesu appears prophetically of the Messiah, approximately one hundred times throughout the Scriptures. It has been translated variously by the words salvation, help and deliverance, although these expressions are also employed to translate other Hebrew words.

"Where do we find the NAME?" you ask. Here it Is, beloved: Every time the Old Testament uses the word salvation (especially with the Hebrew suffix meaning "my," "thy," or "his"), with very few exceptions (when the word is impersonal), it is the very same word [*Yesu*] used in Matthew 1:21. (*Yeshua in the Tenach*, Arthur E. Glass).

SALVATION IS YESU

The *Oxford English Dictionay*, under the etymology of the name "Jesus," draws the connection between the Hebrew noun YSW`H (*salvation, deliverance*) and the proper name YSW` (vol. 5: p. 573). *Thayer's Greek English Lexicon of the New Testament* presents the same conclusion, stating that "writers gave the name the force of YSW`H, see Mt. 1: 21, of. Sir. 46: 1 [apocraphal book Sirach= Ecclesiasticus, not Ecclesiastes] ..." (p. 300). This view was also taken by Dr. Edward Robinson, professor of Biblical literature (instructor in Hebrew in Andover Seminary) who stated that Joshua's original name was HWS` (Numbers 13:8,16), changed by Moses to YHWS` (Numbers 13:16; 1Chronicles 7:27): "After the exile he is called YSW` ...Neh. 8:17; whence the Greek *Iesou[s]*. This last form YSW` differs little from the abstract YSW`H, *help, deliverance, salvation*, and seems to have been so understood ...Matt. 1:22 ..." (*Greek and English Lexicon of the New Testament*, p. 348). In Matthew 1: 21-23, Yesu = Yahweh-Salvation (Saviour), *viz.*, "God with us."

The Hebrew word for salvation, YSW`H (Yeshu`h), is synomymous with the name YSW` (Yesu) and may have been pronounced exactly the same (prior to diacritical points). The Messiah's name is clearly seen in the

Hebrew spelling of *salvation*. This is attested to by many scholars. Anyone who is learned in the Hebrew Scriptures, such as the Pharisees were, would immediately (if not prejudice) draw the comparison between YSW` and YSW`H, and consequently recognize the latter as a reference to the Messiah. So, for logical and practical exegesis, we will translate it by "Yesu" in the Old Testament passages where it appears.

SEVENED

In Psalm 91:14-16 God says, "Because he hath set his love upon me, therefore will I deliver him: I will set him on high [אשגבהו: 'I will exalt him,' *viz.* catching up] BECAUSE HE HATH KNOWN MY NAME. He shall call upon me, and I will answer him: I will be with him in trouble: I will deliver him, and honour [כבד: *glorify*] him. With long life [length of days: *viz. eternal life*] will I satisfy him, and shew him my *Salvation* [Yesu]." In verse 16, "satisfy" is from the Hebrew *sb`* (*saba*), from *sheba* literally *seven*, i.e. "the cardinal number seven (as the sacred full one)." (*A Concise Dictionary of the Words in the Hebrew Bible*, Strong's). The meaning of satisfy comes from the *fullness* or *completeness* of seven. To be *sevened*, is to be made complete, or perfectly fulfilled. God's number of perfection is seven. God created man in the sixth day and rested on the seventh. In the millenniums of time we are rapidly approaching the Day of Yahweh, a millennial day, a 1,000 year Sabbath. To be sevened means to be part of YaHWeH's kingdom in that day. He will "seven" you, i.e. include you in his great Sabbath kingdom, because of your affinity to his name and his commandments (cf. 1John 2:3-4).

The Hebrew sentence is made up of clusters of words and letters. Each cluster consists of a stem with prefixes and suffixes. In the last half of verse 16, we find these two clusters: ואראהו and בישועתי (WARAHW and BYSW`TY). Do you recognize the Saviour's name in the second cluster? If we drop the inflections we will view the stem, YSW`T, in its construct state. The absolute state is YSW`H. In the English translation the clusters would read *and-i-see-him with-yesu-my* (with my Yesu). The word which was originally translated "shew" (R'H), should be translated "see," as was done in Job 10:15. It means to literally see. Thus, "and I see him with my Yesu."

In this and other passages the translators evidently failed to recognize YSW`H as a name, which would then have been transliterated as Yesu, and thus rendered it as an event (salvation) rather than a person. Isaiah 62:11 speaks of Salvation, YS` (variant of Yesu) as a person, using the terms His, and Him. This and many other prophetic verses using the word "salvation" are actually direct references to Yesu.

EYES OF THE SPIRIT IN YESU

In context with prophecy the rendering of Psalm 91:16 is, "With length of days [eternal life] I will *seven* him, and I [will] see him with [or by means of] my Yesu." YHWH (Yahweh) will be looking at us through the eyes of Yesu. How is this possible? In Isaiah 43:10-11, Yahweh says, "before me there was no God formed, neither shall there be after me. **I, even I, am YHWH; and beside me there is no Saviour [Ys`: variant of Yesu]**." Yet in Luke 2:11 an angel makes the announcement, "For unto you is born this day in the city of David a Saviour, which is Christ the Lord [Messiah YHWH]." He was not another Saviour, but YHWH in Christ. Yesu is YHWH the Saviour. Yesu said, "If you believe not that *I am* ... [same words YHWH spoke to Moses 'I AM' - Exodus 3:14] ...You shall die in your sins." (John 8:24). Christ was declaring himself to be YHWH the Saviour. He said, "I and my Father are one." (John 10:30); And, "he that hath seen me hath seen the Father." (John 14:9). If Yesu's hand is the Father's hand (John 10:28-30) then Yesu's eyes are the Father's eyes, and YaHWeH will see us with or through his Yesu in the day of the *seven* (the millennium).

Behold, God my *Yesu*; I will trust, and not be afraid: for *Yah*, *Yahweh* is my strength and my song; he also is become my *Yesu*.

Therefore with joy shall ye draw water out of the wells of *Yesu*. [cf. John 4:14; 7:37-39].

And in that day shall ye say, Praise *Yahweh*, call upon his name, declare his doings among the people, make mention that *his name is exalted.* (Isaiah 12:2-4).

Plead my cause, O *Yahweh*, with them that strive with me ... and stand up for mine help ... say unto my soul, I am thy *Yesu* (Psalm 35:1-3).

Yahweh is my strength and my song, and is become my *Yesu*....

I will praise thee: for thou hast heard me, and art become my *Yesu*.

The stone which the builders refused is become the *head* [Hebrew, *rosh*: "top"] of the corner [i.e. the "capstone," cf. 1 Peter 2:6, "cheif cornerstone," from Greek *akron*, "top," and *gonia*, "corner"].

This is *Yahweh's* doing; it is marvelous in our eyes. (Psalm 118:14, 21-23; cf. 1 Peter 2:1-10).

Sing unto *Yahweh* a new song; Sing unto *Yahweh*, all the earth.

sing unto *Yahweh*, bless his name; Proclaim his *Yesu* from day to day.

Declare his glory among the nations, his marvelous works among all the peoples. (Psalm 96:1-3, *Masoretic Text*).

This marvelous work is that YHWH is become Yesu the chief corner stone which the builders rejected. Those high and mighty Pharisees rejected the name of Yahweh by forbidding its use, just as the religions of today have rejected the name of Yesu, and thus cast aside the capstone that they might build their own religious structure. But the Scripture says, "Except YHWH build the house, They labour in vain that build it." (Psalm 127:1).

Please read the following important Scripture verses containing the name Yesu (in the noun YSW`H). While reading, remember to read "Yesu" in the place of *salvation*, and "Yahweh" where *the LORD* appears in capital letters in the *King James Version*. Be sure to read, Genesis. 49:18; 1 Chronicles 16:23; Psalm 13:5-6; 14:7; 62:1-3; 69:29-30; 70:4-5; 78:22; 98:2-3; 116:13, "**I will take the cup of Yesu, and call upon the name of Yahweh**"; 119:155, 166; 149:4; Isaiah 25:9; 33:2, 5-6; 49:6; 52:7, 10; 62:1. Read also the following two verses which contain YS` (variant of Yesu) Isaiah 62:11 and Isaiah 59:16. If you don't have a Bible it is important to get one. If you cannot afford one, check the thrift stores. It is important that you read these verses.

> We will rejoice in thy *Yesu*, and in the name of our God we will set up banners: *Yahweh* fulfill all thy petitions.... we will remember the name of *Yahweh* our God (Psalm 20:5-7).

> And they that know thy name will put their trust in thee: for thou, *Yahweh*, hast not forsaken them that seek thee. ...

> I will rejoice with thy *Yesu*. The heathen are sunk down in the pit that they made: in the net which they hid is their own foot taken.

> ...the wicked is snared in the work of his own hands. (Psalm 9:10, 14-16).

IDOLATROUS NAMES ARE BLASPHEMY

In essence, mankind has rejected the name of God and invented a name which was pleasing to them, *the work of their own hands*. They have essentially set up an idol. To change the name of God is probably the greatest sin (mistake) which mankind has ever committed. To knowingly call God by a made up name is an horrendous blasphemy.

Like other Hebrew proper names, the name of God is more than a mere distinguishing title. It represents the Hebrew conception of the divine nature or character and of the relation of God to His people. It represents the Deity as He is known to His worshippers, and stands for all those attributes which He bears in relation to them and which are revealed to them through His activity on their behalf....

It can readily be understood, therefore, how the divine name is often spoken of as equivalent to the divine presence or power or glory.... The devout Israelite will not take the name of a false god upon his lips (Ex. 23:13; Josh. 23:3; Ps. 16:4). To make mention of YHWH's name is to assert confidence in His strength and present and efficient aid.... (*The Jewish Encyclopedia*, vol. 9: p. 160).

For the Semitic peoples, an unnamed thing was a nonexistent thing; names were considered to identify and describe the very being and function of their bearers ...A man's name represented him wholly ...To know a name was to be able to exercise influence over the owner by using it. To change a man's name was to show one's power and authority over him ...To cut off a man's name was the same as destroying him...

In religious matters, knowledge of the name of a god was considered the most effective way of establishing contact with him. (*New Catholic Encyclopedia*, vol. 10: p. 200).

If changing a man's name shows one's power and authority over him, what have men proclaimed by changing God's name? When cutting off a man's name is the same as destroying him, does anyone dare cut off God's name? If knowledge of the name of God puts one in contact with him, what happens if the wrong name is used?

This is the most serious problem that a person may ever encounter, for if we are calling on a counterfeit name, who knows what god or what spirit will answer?

Will you be held accountable for praying in the wrong name? Is there a problem with using the name *Jesus*, if you are doing it sincerely? Will you be saved in the name of *Jesus*?

These are questions you must ask yourself, and you must also answer them. Continue your research. You have the facts, so you have the answers within yourself. All you need to do is yield to the Holy Spirit, *change your mind* (repent) and *turn away* from the fabricated false names and erroneous gospel.

BLESSING IS NOT PROOF

Some people contend that *Jesus* must be the correct name, otherwise why are prayers being answered, and people healed and converted in that name?

Is answered prayer real evidence toward the validity of *Jesus'* name? No, answered prayer is not a proof of God's acceptance and blessing (cf. Deuteronomy 13:1-3; Jeremiah 44:15-19).

The prayers of witches and devil worshippers are being answered too. When a Rosicrucian learns to command the Force, even his prayers are answered. I know this from my own personal past experience, prior to repentance in 1975. I was very fortunate that God rescued me and opened my eyes to the true light.

For most people answered prayer may seem to be the end of the search, the seal of God's recognition and approval upon their lifestyles and religious practices. Satan will blind a person's mind, causing him to become self-satisfied and self-assured, making it difficult for that person to see God's real intent upon his life. But, for the lover of truth and the diligent seeker, answered prayer can create an authentic desire to really know and serve the one true God. Answered prayer develops the faith necessary to pass through greater levels of truth and acceptance.

Yahweh can lead a person out of the deepest darkness of ignorance through answered prayer.

A person may allow answered prayer to draw him closer to God and truth, or he may allow Satan to use it to administer deceit. The same answered prayer may affect two people differently; one positively, the other negatively. Personal intent and disposition of the petitioner will bear heavily upon the consequences and outcome. The way in which a person is affected depends greatly upon his own attitudes, ambitions and intentions.

Some prayers are answered by Yahweh, others may be forged by Satan or even appropriated by him.

Satan could use a divinely answered prayer to deceive the recipient into thinking he has it all, thus ending his search and stunting his spiritual growth. Yet God could cause a demonic counterfeit prayer-answer to backfire and inspire a search for deeper truths to lead one out of darkness, thus thwarting the Adversary's plan.

God can use answered prayer to guide a willing subject into His word and, thus, by the power of the Holy Spirit, can communicate the knowledge necessary to receive the revelation of His name and other facts to His truly chosen people. "Many are called but few are chosen" (Matthew 22:14; for example, see 1Peter 3:20, only eight saved from the flood; Luke 4:25-27, one saved out of many).

THE WRONG COMFORTER

The Adversary constantly works to counterfeit the true message of God.

Satan, as Lucifer, said, "I shall be like the Most High, I shall sit also upon the *Mount of the Congregation.*" That is *Har Moad* in Hebrew, and *Har Megeddo* or *Armageddon* in Greek. In this prophecy of Isaiah 14:12-14, and in many other Scripture verses, the Adversary makes it clear that he will infiltrate the congregation and be worshiped as God and Saviour. His struggle to do so is literally the battle of Armageddon.

The Mystery of Iniquity, better translated "the Secret of Lawlessness," spoken of in 2Thessalonians 2:3-12, is Satan imitating and appearing as Christ. We see in 2Corinthians 11:14-15, that this secret applies to both Satan and his duped followers, masquerading as servants of Christ and ministers of righteousness. Scripture says the appearance of Antichrist is according to the "energy" of Satan (2Thessalonians 2:9, from the Greek).

The Luciferian initiation is when someone receives the energy (*energeia*) of the satans, believing it is the light of God. This person will be in the service of the Antichrist ("instead-of-Christ") believing he is doing a service to God (cf. John 16:2-3).

We must be extremely cautious, alert and aware, for the secret of lawlessness, the mystery of iniquity, is undoubtedly at work in our time.

(*The Yod of God: Returning His Name, Recovering His Remnant*, Kox).

STRONG DELUSION

In a North-Eastern Wisconsin church where God had chosen to reveal his name, this prophecy came forth, "I have not revealed my name unto the world but unto those that love me." And for those who have not received the love of the truth, "God shall send them strong delusion [*working of error*] that they should believe the lie." (2Thessalonians 2:10-11). The Jehovah-Jesus error is the biggest mistake of all time, these names being the result of fraudulent copy, mistranslation, misunderstanding and mispronunciation.

Jesus is not the same name as Iesu (Yesu). The J, because of its modern application changes the name completely. Yah,

Yahu, Yahweh, Yesu (and perhaps Yeshua) are all variations of the divine name, but Jesus is totally unrelated. Consider how Harry, Harold and Herald are variants of a name, but change the H to a J and Herald becomes Jerald, a completely different name. Harry and Jerry are unrelated names.

From one language to another it is important to transliterate proper names so that they do not lose their correct pronunciation. This proves itself in the Bible where names are carried over from the Hebrew into the Greek: Abraham, Amos, Daniel, Yisrael, Yacob, Yeremiah, Yob, Yoel, Yonah, Yoseph, Michael, Naaman, Pharoah, Pharisee, Rachel, Rahab, Ruth, Solomon, etc. Except for the names beginning in Y, all of these are recognizable in English. Even Baal and Satan, the names of the Devil remain unchanged. But the Serpent made a little hook shape with his tail and the Y (Hebrew and Greek I) became a J. Then in the passing of time the y-sound hardened into the dzh of the modern English J, and the name of Yesu (Iesu) was lost to the made up name Jesus. In the meanwhile, the name of Satan continues unmolested by the changing times.

The English J does not necessarily have to follow after the traditional J sound. The name "Yon" appears in writing as Jon. A stranger seeing this name in writing could not properly address the man. But to his immediate friends and to those whom he has chosen to disclose his name, there would be no problem, when they saw the name in writing they would simply pronounce the J with its original Y sound and Jon would come out "Yon." Keep this in mind, and when you see the name Jesus, remembering it should always be pronounced "yay-soo."

If the Messiah's name had been Jesus, as traditionally pronounced in English, the Hebrew equivalent may have been *DZYZS* or *DSYZS*. Ancient languages had no J sound and thus Hebrew had no letter to represent the J. The Greek may have been *Zisos*: (dzees-us; Greek z=dz), since neither of these languages has a J. Modern Hebrew uses a *Gimel* (G) with a diacritical mark above it to indicate the English J sound (since it is sometimes necessary today, but was not so in earlier times). The Saviour's name begins with Yod, which never receives a J sound. The Biblical spelling of the Messiah's name can not be pronounced Jesus.

DON'T TAKE THE BAIT

Yesu said, "No man comes to the Father [YHWH] except through me." (John 14:6). When you understand the "oneness" you can realize the full significance of this statement. YHWH is in Yesu; Yesu and YHWH are one; When you see Yesu you see YHWH (2Corinthians 5:19; John 10:30; 14:7, 9, 10). We must come through Yesu, he is the way, the truth, and the life (John 14:6).

Yesu came to manifest YaHWeH's name, which at that time had not been spoken in public for several hundred years (John 17:6, 26). He worked his miracles in the name of YHWH (John 10:25). Christ did not sin, neither was "guile" found in his mouth (1Peter 2:22). This word *guile* is from a Greek word meaning "decoy." What is a decoy? It is a bait or lure that is meant to fool the one it is set before. It is presented as the real thing but is a lifeless imitation. The Jews of that time had ceased to use the name of YHWH. They had substituted the imitations of *Adonai* and *Kyrios*. Yesu would not use these decoys but openly professed the name of YHWH (Psalm 22:22) though it meant certain death. Capital punishment was inflicted upon anyone pronouncing the sacred name.

THEY WILL HATE YOU FOR MY NAME

Yesu said, the world will hate you "*because of my name,*" and "the time cometh that whosoever killeth you will think that he doeth God service." (Read John 15:18-27; 16:1-3). They killed him, they will also hate us and even seek to kill us if we use his blessed name. Yesu said your parents, brothers, relatives and friends will betray you; and some will be put to death; "And ye shall be hated of all men for my name's sake [Greek: '*because of my name*']" (Luke 21:16-17). Hated because of his real name, not a decoy. Can we continue to use the names *Jehovah* and *Jesus*? "He that will love life, and see good days, let him refrain his tongue from evil, and his lips that they speak no *guile* [decoy]." (1Peter 3:10).

The major portion of Modern Christianity constitutes the Church of Antichrist, promoting Jehovah and Jesus, the false Gospel and the false Jesus image. Most are so indoctrinated they will hate you if you proclaim the truth, because it exposes their *sacred* falsehoods.

The name of Jesus is a decoy. Antichrist means instead of Christ. Jesus is instead-of-christ. Will you be saved without believing in the name of Yesu? You decide (examine John 3:18). If you are ashamed of Yesu's words and you deny his name, he will deny you (see Matthew 10:33; Mark 8:38; Luke 9:26).

Yesu would not conform to the traditions of the Pharisees, neither should we follow the pattern of modern religions. We must declare the name of Yesu, Messiah YHWH. "Yahweh is the true God, he is the living God, and the everlasting king." (Jeremiah 10:10).

When Thomas beheld the living Christ, he declared, "My *Yahweh* and my God" (John 20:28). There was no doubt in his mind that Yesu is YHWH the Saviour. Knowing the truth, can we substitute any other name for that of Yahweh the Saviour? Yesu (*Yahweh the Saviour*) is the only name by which we must be saved (see Acts 4:10-12).

NO SUBSTITUTE

Even in the face of death the Messiah would not substitute a decoy for the name of YaHWeH. He knew the law of the Sanhedrin: "The prohibition of blasphemy, for which capital punishment is prescribed, refers only to the Name proper — YHWH (Soferim iv., end; comp. Sanh. 662)." (*The Jewish Encyclopedia*, vol. 9: p. 163). "According to Sanh. vii. 5, actual blasphemy is committed only when the blasphemer really pronounces the Tetragrammaton ('Shem ha-Meyuhad'; comp. Sifra, Emor, xix, [ed. Weiss, p. 104d])." (*ibid*. vol. 11: p. 263). It is implied in Jewish Talmud that Yesu was executed for pronouncing the name of Yahweh: "The blasphemer is punished only if he utters [the divine] Name... the witnesses are examined by means of a substitute for the divine Name. ... when the trial was finished, the accused was not executed on this evidence, but all persons were removed [from court], and the chief witness was told, 'state literally what you heard'. Thereupon he did so, [using the divine Name]. The Judges then arose and rent their garments, which rent not to be re-sewn. The second witness stated: 'I too have heard thus' [but not uttering the divine Name], and the third says: 'I too heard thus'." (*The Babylonian Talmud* [Seder Nezikin, in 4 vols.] vol. 3, "Sanhedrin", p. 378).

There is no doubt that Yesu used the divine name in such recorded instances as John 8:24, 58-59; 18:5-6 ("I AM" is the equivalent of the name YHWH spoken in the first person [grammatical expression] cf. Exodus 3:14-15).

He may even have uttered the name at his own trial, as recorded in the Bible. "The Jews often used the word *power* to substitute for pronouncing the Sacred Name." (*The Memorial Name Yahweh*, p. 58). At his trial, Yesu said, "Hereafter shall ye see the Son of man sitting on the right hand of POWER, and coming in the clouds of heaven." (Matthew 26:64). Hearing this the high priest rent his clothes and declared, "He hath spoken blasphemy; what further need have we of witnesses? Behold, now ye have heard his blasphemy. What think ye? They answered and said, He is guilty of death." (Matthew 26:65-66; cf. Mk. 14:61-65).

In Hebrew idiom, the right hand was the position of authority. To be at one's right hand signified taking his place in all matters of authority, to exercise his power and express his will (e.g. Genesis 41:40-44; cf. Matthew 28:18). "The Scripture generally imputes to God's right hand all the effects of his omnipotence." (*Cruden's Pocket Dictionary of Bible Terms*, p. 142). The high priest and the Jewish Pharisees evidently understood Yesu as saying, Hereafter you will see the Son of man in place of YHWH, coming in the clouds of heaven. They knew their Scriptures well, and Psalm 118 must have been ringing in their ears:

> YHWH is my strength and song, and is become my *Yesu*. The voice of rejoicing and *Yesu* is in the tabernacles of the righteous the right hand of YHWH doeth valiantly. The right hand of

YHWH is exalted: the right hand of YHWH doeth valiantly. (vv. 14-16).

I will praise thee: for thou hast heard me, and art become my *Yesu*; The stone which the builders refused is become the *head* [*rosh*: "top"] of the corner [i.e. the "capstone"]. (vv. 21-22; cf. Luke 20:9-19).

Hosanna [save now], I beseech thee, YHWH: send prosperity now, I beseech thee, YHWH. Blessed be he that cometh in the NAME of YHWH. (vv. 25-26).

Just a short time earlier, they had heard the great multitudes crying to the son of David, "Hosanna, Blessed is he that cometh in the name of Yahweh." (see Matthew 21:9; Mark 11:9-10; Luke 19:38-39). The name of Yahweh had been concealed by the Pharisees who used the substitute *Adonay*. The multitudes may have been using this substitute, but surely Yesu had revealed to them the proper pronunciation of the HaShem, the Tetragrammaton.

The Pharisees had heard the children "crying in the temple and saying to the son of David, '*Hosanna*' [i.e. 'save now']" (Matthew 21:15). They had angrily commanded Yesu to rebuke them (v. 16; cf. Luke 19:39). And now this same Yesu, from his own lips, was as much as telling them, I am YHWH's Right Hand. They had heard what Yesu said, and they knew that YHWH's Right Hand was the Messiah, the Saviour (see Psalm 48:10; 60:5; 80:17-18; 98:1-3, *salvation* = Yesu; 108:6; 110:1; 138:7). Although evidence showed Yesu to be the Messiah they could not accept him without breaking Scripture; he had to die.

MASTER OF THE NAME

The fact that Yesu worked his miracles in the name of YHWH (Yahweh) is even attested to in Jewish folklore. "There was found the popular notion that if [Yesu] of Nazareth had been able to perform the miracles ascribed to him by Christians, including his accomplishment of walking dryshod on the waters of the Sea of Galilee, it was only because he had made himself master of the 'secret' name of God." (*The Book of Jewish Knowledge*, p. 69). The Jews also stated that Yesu "was regarded as a god and that his name was considered as efficacious as the Tetragrammaton itself, for which it was even substituted." (*The Jewish Encyclopedia*, vol. 12: p. 119). As the Messiah and Right Hand of God, that is the chosen vessel in which the Father resided (2Corinthians 5:19; Colossians 2:9), Yesu worked his miracles in the name of Yahweh (John 10:25). His disciples used his name to work miracles (Mark 16:17-18; Luke 10:17-20; John 14:13; 16:24). If you are chosen and ordained of God you will be conducting your prayers in the name of Yesu (John 15:16) which is actually a direct address to the Father. Every time you pronounce the name of Yesu (yay-soo) you are saying "YHWH help," literally "Yahweh the Saviour." Yahweh is the one who doeth the works (John 14:10).

If it were not for the ancient synagogue practice of substituting *Adonai* for YHWH, followed later by the Greek *Kyrios*, appearing in our English Bibles as LORD, it would be plain to see, by comparing Old and New Testaments, that Yesu is YHWH and that to use his name is to use the name of YHWH. "The oldest LXX [*Septuagint*] manuscripts (fragments) now available to us have the Tetragrammaton written in Hebrew characters in the Greek text." (*The New International Dictionary of New Testament Theology*, vol 2: p. 512). But in the more recent LXX manuscripts, the sacred name is omitted. The word kyrios appears over 9,000 times in the LXX. "In the overwhelming majority of cases *kyrios* replaces the Hebrew proper name of God, the Tetragrammaton *YHWH*." (*ibid.*).

In light of the previously examined evidence, and the fact that *Kyrios* replaces *YHWH* in the *Septuagint*, it is plain to see that in the New Testament *Kyrios* should be translated *YHWH* (Yahweh) where the context warrants it.

...God exalted Him and gave to Him who was called [*Yesu*] at His birth a new name —"the name that is above every name, so that at the name of

[*Yesu*] every knee should bend of those in heaven, on earth, and under the earth, and every tongue should confess to the glory of God the Father that [*Yesu*] Christ is *KYRIOS* [i.e. *YHWH*]" (Philp. 2:5-11). The "name above every name" can be only the unutterable name of "Yahweh", whom every being in the universe must adore, and *kyrios* "Lord" is here the Greek for *adonai*, the word substituted for *Yahweh*; cf. also Is. 45:22-23) ...By thus identifying [*Yesu*] Christ, the Lord of the N.T., with "the Lord, i.e., Yahweh, of the O.T., several passages of the O.T. which speak of "the LORD" (Yahweh) are applied in the N.T. to our "Lord," [*Yesu*] Christ: compare, e.g., Mt. 3:3; Mk. 1:3; Luke. 3:4; Jn. 1:23 with Is. 40:3; or Rom. 10:13 with Joel 2:32 [Masoretic text 3:5]; or 1Cor. 1:31 with Jer. 9:23 [M.T. 9:22] or 1Pet. 2:3 with Ps. 33:8-9; 34:8-9; or 1Pet. 3:14 with Is. 8:13; etc. In 1Cor. 10:9, where there is an allusion to, but not a direct quotation from Nm. 21:5; Ps. 95:8-9; [Ex. 17:7], the word "Christ" is explicitly substituted for "Yahweh." Thus, the term, "Lord," as applied to Christ, takes on a special theological significance. ...In order to be a Christian one must acknowledge that [*Yesu*] is the Lord [i.e.*Yahweh*] (1Cor. 12:3; cf. 1Jn. 4:1-ff) an acknowledgment which can only be made under the influence of the Holy Spirit (1Cor. 12:3). (*Encyclopedic Dictionary of the Bible*, p. 1374).

GURDIAN AND KEEPER OF THE BREAD

The title "Lord" cannot always be translated as YHWH. Careful discretion must be used. Sometimes the term lord is even applied to man. Our English word Lord is a quite fitting title for Yesu: The title is derived from Middle English: *lord, laverd, loverd*, from Anglo-Saxon: *hlaford*, for *hlafweard*, i.e. bread keeper, from *hlaf* : bread, loaf, and *weard*: keeper, guard (see *ward*). Ward:

Middle English: *wardien*, Anglo-Saxon: *weardian*: to *keep or to guard*. Warden: Old French & French: *gardien*, Middle English: *guardian*. (*Webster's New International Dictionary*, 2nd ed. Unabridged, p. 1459, "Lord"; p. 2874 "ward", "warden"). According to its etymology, the actual literal meaning of "Lord" is, "***Guardian and Keeper of the Bread***." Read John 6:26-64, then recall the words of the model prayer, "Give us this day our daily bread."

YAHWEH IS YESU

Since the Greek *Kyrios*, in most cases represents the name YHWH, when the New Testament refers to the Father as "the Lord," or to the Messiah as "Yesu is Lord," or "Yesu is the Lord," it should almost always be translated Yahweh, for YHWH. "The word *Kyrios* [Lord] obviously stands for 'Yahweh' in such expressions as 'Kyrios, your (or my) God'." (*Encyclopedic Dictionary of the Bible*, p. 1371).

> The title *Lord* (Greek kyrios) is used of [*Yesu*] Christ almost seven hundred times. In combination with [*Yesu*] and Christ, the title has a threefold significance: [*Yesu*] is Saviour; Christ is the anointed of God; as Lord, He is master of life. The title *kyrios* was also used as an equivalent of Yahweh in the old Greek translation of the Old Testament, and it is so used in the New Testament as well ...Therefore an identification of [*Yesu*] Christ with Yahweh Himself is involved in this title of *kyrios* or "Lord." (*Harper Study Bible [RSV]* p. 1448).

If the pronunciation of the names had not been hidden, through time and translation, there could be no mistaking the Oneness of God and the divinity of Christ.

The formula developed by the early Church father, Tertullian, actually confirmed the Deity of Christ while re-affirming the Oneness of the Godhead. Most Trinitarians believe in the Oneness, although the terminology has become a stumbling block for many.

NOT ONE YOD SHALL PASS AWAY

Referring to the law and the prophets, i.e. the Old Testament Scriptures, Yesu said, not one "jot" (*iota*; *yod*) or one "title" shall pass away as long as heaven and earth remain (Matthew 5:17-18). This is a direct reference to the scribal accuracy of Hebrew Scripture.

The word "jot" is taken from the Greek *iota* (*Koine Greek* pronunciation: *yota*), which is derived from the Semitic *yod*. "According to the Masoretes [the Scribes] there are 66,420 yods in the text of the Hebrew Scriptures." (*Assemblies of Yahweh Correspondence Course*, lesson 1: p. 2). Not one "iota," i.e. "yod," shall pass from the Scriptures until all things be fulfilled. All things will not be fulfilled until after Satan and his rebels have been destroyed in the lake of fire (Revelation 20:10, 14-15; cf. Ezekiel 28:18-19).

The most important thing written in the law and the prophets is the name of God and Saviour. The first letter in God's name is a *yod* (represented by I or Y) IHUH or YHWH; ISU` or YSW`, Greek *Iesou*. Yesu said that not one "yod" would pass from the Hebrew Scriptures. The "yod" has not passed away. The names YHWH (Yahweh) and YSW` (Yesu) still appear in the Hebrew Scriptures today, and will until the end of time. Heaven and earth have not passed away. *Jehovah* is not God and the Saviour's name is not *Jesus*.

ENGLISH CHANGED GOD'S NAME

It is through the Modern English J that the sacred names have been changed and counterfeited. The English speaking nations, Great Britain and the United States, are guilty of taking away the "yod" and changing the name of God. The Ephraimites were noted for mispronouncing names (e.g. Judges 12:1-6): Great Britain represents Ephraim. Manasseh means "forgetting" or "one who forgets." The U.S.A. represents Manasseh. Ephraim and Manasseh were half-tribes which together made up the tribe of Joseph. The boundary between the two was uncertain. In ancient times they did not drive out the pagan Canaanites from before them as commanded but rather allowed them to dwell in the land (Joshuah 16:9-10; 17:7-13).

When Hezekiah sent word to Ephraim and Manasseh that they should come to the house of Yahweh at Jerusalem to celebrate the Passover, they laughed and scorned (2Chronicles 30:1, 9-10). The Ephraimites broke God's covenant and law, introducing their own gods (Psalm 78:9-11; 1Kings 11:26; 12:25-30; Hosea 4:17; 5:9, 12; 6:10). So, YHWH has forsaken Ephraim (cf. Deut. 31:16-17). They shall not dwell in YHWH's land, but "shall return to Egypt" (Hosea 9:3, cf. viz. around 1900, the UK and US adapted an architectural Egyptianization). Their sacrifices shall be as the bread of mourners, "all that eat thereof shall be polluted," and "thorns shall be in their tabernacles." (vv. 4-6). Their prophets are fools, they have "corrupted," therefore the glory of Ephraim shall "fly away like a bird," and "there shall not be a man left." (vv. 7-13).

> O generation, see ye the word of YHWH. Have I been a wilderness unto Israel? a land of darkness? wherefore say my people, *We are lords*; we will come no more unto thee? ...
>
> Also in thy skirts is found the blood of the souls of the poor innocents [*abortions?*] ...
>
> Yet thou sayest, Because I am innocent, surely his anger shall turn from me. Behold, I will plead with thee, because thou sayest, I have not sinned. ...
>
> YHWH hath rejected thy confidences, and thou shalt not prosper in them. (Jeremiah 2:31-37).

Which people call themselves lords? The British. Because of their corruption of the gospel, they are to be rejected by Yahweh. He shall cast down the "crown of pride" and the "drunkards of Ephraim" are trodden under feet (Isaiah 28:1-3).

> The fortress also shall cease from Ephraim... and there shall be desolation. Because **thou hast forgotten thy God Yesu**... therefore shalt thou plant pleasant plants, and shalt set it with *strange slips*: In the day shalt thou make thy plant to grow, and in the morning shalt thou make thy seed to flourish: but the harvest shall be a heap in the day of grief and of desperate sorrow. (Isaiah 17:3, 9-11).

They have forgotten Yahweh-Yesu and have set their strange slips: the invented names, *Jehovah* and *Jesus*. The harvest shall be a heap of bodies in the valley of Gehenna (see Ezekiel 24:9-10). "There shall not be a man left." (Hosea 9:12). "The crown of pride... shall be trodden under feet." (Isaiah 28:3). "The fortress also shall cease from Ephraim... and there shall be desolation." (Isaiah 17:3, 9). The harlot Great Britain is headed for the fall, but along with her will be her sister harlot, the United States.

> Woe to the multitude of many people, which make a noise like the noise of the seas; and to the rushing of nations, that make a rushing like the rushing of mighty waters!
>
> The nations shall rush like the rushing of many waters: but God shall rebuke them, and they shall flee far off, and shall be chased as the chaff of the mountains before the wind, and like a rolling thing before the whirlwind.
>
> And behold at eveningtide trouble; and before the morning *he is not* [*RSV*: "**they are no more**"]. This is the portion of them that spoil us, and the lot of them that rob us.
>
> Woe to the land shadowing with wings...
>
> (Isaiah 17:12-14; 18:1).

DESTRUCTION OF THE UNITED STATES

The multitude of many peoples: the U.S.A. has people from all nations and tongues. *Noise like the noise of the seas, like the rushing of mighty waters*: the sound of automobile traffic rushing by. *They shall flee far off … like a rolling thing before the whirlwind*: destruction, perhaps nuclear. *At eveningtide trouble*: according to God's timetable it is now eveningtide. *Before the morning they are no more*: this may indicate the total destruction of the United States, i.e. wiped right off the map, for *the land shadowing with wings* could easily represent the United States with her "wings" of the so-called eagle (*viz.* phoenix).

Read Deuteronomy 32. *Yeshurun* (Hebrew, *righteous one*; LXX, *beloved*) forsook God, YHWH, who made him, "and lightly esteemed the Rock his Yesu." (v. 15). "They sacrificed to demons, and not to God; to gods, which they had never known, which had started up, new and fictitious, of which their fathers had no knowledge…" (v. 17, *The Septuagint Bible in the translation of Charles Thomson*). Thou hast forgotten the God that formed thee, i.e. YHWH (v. 18). Who are the gods that came newly up? Jehovah and Jesus are certainly among them, being only a few hundred years old.

Deuteronomy 32:20 says, "they are a very froward generation". *Froward*, is taken from the Hebrew *tahpukah*: a *perversity* or *fraud*. The *Jehovah-Jesus* error is the biggest fraud of all time. "They have moved me to jealousy with that which is not God" (v. 21). *Jehovah* is not God, neither is his name *Jesus*. "Their rock is not as our Rock" (v. 31). The day of their destruction is near, "their power is gone, and there is none shut up, or left… Where are their gods, their rock in whom they trusted?" (vv. 35-37). For those who are trusting falsely in the misnomers of Jehovah and Jesus, YHWH says, "I, even I, am he, and there is no god with me." (v. 39). Yahweh-Yesu is One God alone.

Deuteronomy 32:48, and following, describe how Moses was not allowed to enter the Promised Land, "because ye sanctified me not." What error did Moses make? "He smote the rock twice" (Numbers 20:7-12; cf. Exodus 17:5-7). Perhaps the English speaking people have smote the Rock twice, by taking away the iota (yota/yod) from the name Yahweh and from the name Yesu. This distorted the holy name of "our Rock." Because of this fraud the power of God is not with them. Although individuals, a few, may be saved, as a whole the U.S. and Britain are doomed to destruction.

NAME FALSIFIED BY THE GOYIM

Yahweh's name is being "profaned among the *goyim*" by the House of Israel, U.S. And U.K. (Ezekiel 36:20-22). How? By the misspelling and mispronunciation, God's holy name has been taken in vain and counted as nothing, in violation of the third commandment. "YHWH will *not acquit* him that taketh his name falsely." (Exodus 20:7, *falsely*: Heb. *shav*, especially *guile*: decoy). To falsify his name and make it a decoy is a direct violation of the commandment.

PUBLISH THE TRUE NAME

It is the duty of all God's people to "publish the name" (see Deuteronomy 32:3; Isaiah 52:7). If you are a minister or a pastor you must try to reveal the truth to the flock, and pray that they will receive it. If they reject it and cast you out of their midst, remember what Yesu said: You will be persecuted and hated for my name's sake, that is, *"because of my name"* (Matthew 5:11; 10:22-23; 24:9; Mark 13:13; Luke 21:12, 17; John 15:20-21). You must take a stand for Yahweh-Yesu and his commandmants, including the Sabbath. You dare not continue to speak and teach falsehoods, or you will be found a liar (1John 2:1-6).

Have you ever had anyone call you by the wrong name? After a few times it gets quite irritating. You would probably look for a way of gently correcting that person, and if they still persisted in calling you by the wrong name, it may even spoil a chance for a friendship. Would you purposely call someone by the wrong name if you knew their proper name? To see the

Messiah's birth certificate look to the Greek New Testament, Matthew 1:21. There is recorded the unchangeable name of the Saviour as given from heaven: *Iesou*, Yesu (less inflectional n).

Yesu said, "Struggle to enter in at the strait gate: for many, I say unto you, will seek to enter in, and shall not be able." (Luke 13:24). He is not talking about those who do not care and who willingly and knowingly rebel against God. He says, Many **will seek to enter** in at the *strait* gate but **will not be able to**. They are religious Christian people who are actually seeking to enter the *strait* gate but can not. Why can't they? A strait is a narrow waterway. The strait gate may be a reference to the water baptism, immersion in Yesu's name which is the entrance to the household of YHWH: *baptized* into Christ (Romans 6:3; Galatians 3:27). "No man cometh to the Father but *through* me" (John 14:6). They cannot enter in, though they may try, because their false forms of baptism are merely closet doors. The only door to the sheepfold is Yesu (John 10:7-9). The entrance to the strait gate is immersion in the name of Yesu Christ, which will be followed (or preceded) in the true believer, by the baptism of the Holy Spirit which is the seal of adoption.

Though they sought to enter, in the final hour he shall say to them, "I tell you, I know you not whence ye are; depart from me, all ye workers of iniquity." (Luke 13:27). In this verse "*workers*" is from the Greek *ergates*: a *toiler*, figuratively a *teacher*. And *iniquity* is from *adikia*: *unrighteousness*. In many passages it indicates *deceit*, and can so be translated. Thus the passage in question can be read, "He will speak, saying, I have not known you, where are you from, *get away from me all you teachers of deceit*."

In another place he has said:

> Not every one that saith unto me, Lord, Lord, shall enter into the kingdom of heaven; but he that doeth the will of my Father which is in heaven.
>
> Many will say to me in that day, Lord, Lord, have we not prophesied in thy name? and in thy name have cast out devils? and in thy name done many wonderful works?

And then I will profess unto them, I never knew you: depart from me, ye that work iniquity.

(Matthew 7:21-23).

They will be saying, Lord, Lord, have we not done all these things in your name? And, in essence, he will be saying to them, No you did not. When did you ever use my name? I don't know you, I never heard you call my name. How can you expect me to let you into my household? This passage in Matthew differs from the one just examined in Luke. "Work," is from the Greek, *ergazomai*: *toil* (to *produce*) sometimes translated *minister*; and "iniquity," is from *anomia*: *illegality, without law*. The last part of verse 23 may then be properly read, "*get away from me, you who minister illegally*," or "ministering without the law," i.e. *lawless ones*, viz. modern no-commandment gospel (cf. 2Thessalonians 2:7-8).

The names of Jehovah and Jesus are actually illegal, having been produced outside the law, i.e. not being written in the *Law (Torah) and the Prophets*, the Hebrew Scriptures.

A lady, whom Yesu was dealing with on his name, said, I know that Yesu is the name but I just don't think I can give up the name of Jesus. She prayed for guidance and an answer to her dilemma. Within the next few nights she had a dream in which someone was pursuing her, and a voice spoke saying, "If you like that name so much, I am going to mark you with it forever." Then a hand with long claws reached out and began to gouge the name of Jesus into her back. The interpretation seemed plain enough. She said that she felt the name was from hell and that Satan was gouging it into her for eternity.

Opel Kline, A Pentecostal Minister, when presented with the name of Yesu, became very excited. She said that several years earlier, while praying in the Spirit and speaking in tongues, she began to repeat Yesu, over and over, recalling that she had sounded like a broken record. She felt as though she were calling on the Saviour, even though she was not saying *Jesus*. The experience was so striking that she wrote down the name in hopes of someday finding out what it meant. Upon presentation of the names Yahweh and Yesu, she said God spoke to her warning "Shake not off!"

ONLY ONE SAVING NAME

Acts 4:10-12 tells us there is only one name given under heaven by which we must be saved, the name "Yesu Christ." Remission of sins comes through his name (Acts 2:38; 10:43). The Father's name is Yesu (John 5:43; cf. Psalms 35:1-3). The Son's name is Yesu (Matthew 1:21). The name of the Holy Ghost is Yesu (John 14:26). One Lord, YHWH, and one name (Zechariah 14:9). We are to be baptized in that one name (Matthew 28:19). We are washed, sanctified and justified in the name of Yahweh-Yesu, and by the Spirit of God (1Corinthians 6:11). That you might have life, eternal life, through the name of Yesu (John 20:31). The baptism of Matthew 28:19 and Acts 2:38 is not in the name of Jesus, but in the name of Yesu (yay-soo) Christ. The name Jesus did not exist until modern history.

If you are ready to enter into the strait gate, you must go down into the watery grave with Christ (Romans 6:1-6). Jonah was immersed in a watery hell symbolic of Christ's burial in the tomb (Jonah 2:1-3; Matthew 12:40). When Jonah repented in the belly of the whale, his confession was, "Salvation [Yesu] is of Yahweh." (Jonah 2:9). It takes the guidance of the Holy Spirit to recognize and acknowledge this truth (see 1Corinthians 12:3, cf. 1John 4:1-ff).

We need to believe in truth. Scripture says the truth will make you free. It never says that sincerity will make you free. There are many sincere believers, who are sincerely believing in false doctrines.

Sincerity is not enough to prove that there is a truth. A person may be sincere in believing that he is putting baking powder into the pancake mixture when in reality it is arsenic. This happened in one kitchen. A woman took a baking powder can from the top shelf in her cabinet, was sincere in believing that it was powder. She fed the cakes to her entire family, only to find them all dead. She was arrested for murder. Sincerity is not enough. One must also be right. This is the danger of closing one's heart to the truth. It opens the door for strong delusion. (*Let My People Go*, p. 30).

While in the Holy Land, Pentecostal evangelist, Jonathan Urshan reportedly confronted several orthodox Jews coming from the Wailing Wall (c. 1980). They had been praying for the coming of the Messiah. When asked what is his name? They allegedly replied *Yeshua Ha-Mashiyach*. Urshan said it means Jesus the Messiah. Who knows whether he proprely quoted their Hebrew? They might have said Yesu, or Yeshu, and he may have simply inserted the popular Yeshua, in his re-telling of the story.

Yesu and Yeshua are cognates, but Jesus is a completely different name, like Herbert, Herb, and Herbie are one name, but Robert is another. The name Jesus is the result of misinterpretation and mispronunciation, a new and different name and not the God-given name of the Saviour. No amount of sincerity can change that.

A Jew from Jerusalem, the cameraman mentioned earlier, said they would not refer to Christ by the name Yeshua, but by Yeshu, or Yesu. The Jews in Israel know that Jesus is an erroneous name. All Hebrew dictionaries give the spelling, yod-shin-waw (vav), which depending upon dialect would be Yesu, or Yeshu. It does not spell Yeshua, nor Jesus.

According to a special television documentary the Messianic movement in Jerusalem is now referring to the Messiah as Yeshua, although in one place where the English caption text had Yeshua, the commentator clearly said Yeshu. Yet several of those interviewed recited the name Yeshua. Jews are finally coming to Christ, but it is disturbing that they are now changing his name from Yesu to Yeshua.

Yesu the Messiah is Yesu Christ. Yesu is his name, while Messiah is his title, meaning Christ, "the Anointed."

How can the Jews know the Messiah's name? The Scriptures testify of him.

Then why did they reject him? He had the name of the Messiah, but they did not like his qualities. He did not say what they wanted to hear, so they would not acknowledge him as the

Deliverer of Israel? He was rejected as an impostor, although there is Biblical evidence that the very hierarchy who rejected him knew who he was:

> And one of them, named Caiaphas, being the high priest that same year, said unto them, Ye know nothing at all, Nor consider that it is expedient for us, that one man should die for the people, and that the whole nation perish not. And this spake he not of himself: but being high priest that year, he prophesied that Yesu should die for that nation; And not for that nation only, but that also he should gather together in one the children of God that were scattered abroad. (John 11:49-52)

YAHWEH AND YESU ARE ONE

John the Baptist had come to prepare the way of Yahweh and to point him out to Israel. The one he pointed out was Yesu (YHWH-Saviour) the Messiah (read John 1:23-34; cf. Isaiah 40:3-5). The kingdom is Yahweh's and he is the governor (Psalm 22:28): The kingdom is Yesu's and he is the governor (Isaiah 9:6-7). Yahweh is the first and the last (Isaiah 48:12): Yesu is the first and the last (Revelation 1:17). Yahweh will come with flames of fire to punish them that have not called upon his name (Isaiah 66:15-16; cf. Psalm 79: 6): Yesu will come with flaming fire to punish them that know not God and obey not his gospel, i.e. have not called upon his name, and are not called by his name (2Thessalonians 1:7-9).

When you are called by the name of Yesu, you are called by the name of Yahweh. Psalm 35:1-3 says, "O YHWH...say unto my soul, I AM THY YESU."

The Ark of the Covenant represents the presence of God, with YHWH's name on the ark (1Chronicles 13:6). The headgear worn by the high priest was a crown with the Tetragrammaton inscribed on a golden diadem (Exodus 28:36-37). The anointed high priest typified the Messiah. Christ is the true Ark of God. As our Great High Priest he has a golden band about his head with the name YHWH inscribed upon it. It is his name. Yesu is Yahweh the Saviour.

The day is rapidly approaching, in which all those who have called upon the erroneous name of *Jesus* will finally see that Jesus was a decoy and not God and Saviour. Then, at the name of Yesu, every knee shall bow and every tongue shall confess that "Yesu Christ is Yahweh, the glory of God the Father" (Philppians 2:9-11; cf. Isaiah 45:21-25).

FINAL CONFESSION

The final confession and conviction of all creation is that Yesu is Yahweh.

EPILOGUE

CONCLUSION AND CONVICTION

THE END IS COME

An evil, an only evil, behold, it is come. An end is
come, the end is come: ... behold, it is come. ... the
time is come, the day of trouble is near (Ezekiel
7:5-7).

This is it, **the time of trouble, the day of
tribulation**. Now it is time for all men to put aside their
differences, especially so for Jews and Christians. It is time to
reunite. It is time to be one people of God. We are facing a
critical juncture in God's plan and we need to be ready for it.

Yahweh is the one true God. Yahweh is Yesu the Messiah
and Saviour of Humanity.

New York and the United States are Secret Babylon of
the end times. It is extremely probable that New York will be

destroyed at any moment now. The entire U.S. quite possibly may be destroyed also in the very near future.

You have to decide what to do. You have to make your spiritual decisions, and then you have to make your physical and material decisions. No one can decide for you. It is necessary to weigh the evidence, consider the facts, and calculate the possible consequences.

You will need to do your own research into the facts, then pray for wisdom from God to help you decide the proper stratigy that you must take. This will be difficult for even the unmarried, but those with families it will weigh extremely heavy.

You might be secure enough in your spiritual beliefs to say, I am going to stay right here and face possible suffering and death. I have to die sometime, somewhere, it might as well be here. On the other hand, you might say, I'm not waiting to see what happens. I'm getting out of here while I can. If this whole thing does come down I'm not going to be in the heart of it.

If you drop everything and flee, and then nothing happens, you will be upset that you were rooted out of your home. But if you hang tight and destruction comes, you will be wishing you had made another decision. The choices before you will not be easy. Investigate, pray and choose wisely.

LAST WORD

YAHWEH YESU IN SCRIPTURE

THE FOREVER NAME

Exodus 3:15
And God said moreover unto Moses, Thus shalt thou say unto the children of Israel, **Yahweh** God of your fathers, the God of Abraham, the God of Isaac, and the God of Jacob, hath sent me unto you: **this is my name for ever**, and this is my memorial unto all generations.

GENESIS

Genesis 4:26
And to Seth, to him also there was born a son; and he called his

name Enos: then began men to **call upon the name of Yahweh**.

Genesis 12:8
…and there he built an altar unto **Yahweh**, and **called upon the name of Yahweh**.

Genesis 13:4
Unto the place of the altar, which he had make there at the first: and there Abram **called on the name of Yahweh**.

Genesis 21:33
And Abraham planted a grove in Beersheba, and **called there on the name of Yahweh**, the everlasting God.

Genesis 26:25
And he built an altar there, and **called upon the name of Yahweh**, and pitched his tent there: and there Isaac's servants digged a well.

EXODUS

Exodus 3:15
And God said moreover unto Moses, Thus shalt thou say unto the children of Israel, **Yahweh** God of your fathers, the God of Abraham, the God of Isaac, and the God of Jacob, hath sent me unto you: this is **my name for ever**, and this is my memorial unto all generations.

Exodus 6:3
And I appeared unto Abraham, unto Isaac, and unto Jacob, by the name of God Almighty, but by **my name YAHWEH** was I not known to them.

Exodus 9:16
And in very deed for this cause have I raised thee up, for to shew in thee my power; and that **my name** may be declared throughout all the earth.

Exodus 20:7
Thou shalt not take **the name of Yahweh** thy God in vain; for **Yahweh** will not hold him guiltless that taketh his name in vain.

Exodus 20:24
…in all places **where I record my name** I will come unto thee,

and I will bless thee.

Exodus 23:21
Beware of him, and obey his voice, provoke him not; for he will not pardon your transgressions: for **my name** is in him.

Exodus 33:19
And he said, I will make all my goodness pass before thee, and I will **proclaim the name of Yahweh** before thee; and will be gracious to whom I will be gracious, and will shew mercy on whom I will shew mercy.

Exodus 34:5
And **Yahweh** descended in the cloud, and stood with him there, and **proclaimed the name of Yahweh**.

LEVITICUS

Leviticus 19:12
And ye shall not swear by **my name** falsely, neither shalt thou profane the name of thy God: I am **Yahweh**.

Leviticus 20:3
And I will set my face against that man, and will cut him off from among his people; because he hath given of his seed unto Molech, to defile my sanctuary, and to profane **my holy name**.

Leviticus 22:2
Speak unto Aaron and to his sons, that they separate themselves from the holy things of the children of Israel, and that they profane not **my holy name** in those things which they hallow unto me: I am **Yahweh**.

Leviticus 22:32
Neither shall ye profane **my holy name**; but I will be hallowed among the children of Israel: I am **Yahweh** which hallow you,

Leviticus 24:16
And he that blasphemeth **the name of Yahweh**, he shall surely be put to death, and all the congregation shall certainly stone him: as well the stranger, as he that is born in the land, when he blasphemeth **the name of Yahweh**, shall be put to death.

NUMBERS

Numbers 6:27
And they shall put **my name** upon the children of Israel, and I will bless them.

DEUTERONOMY

Deuteronomy 5:11
Thou shalt not take **the name of Yahweh** thy God in vain: for **Yahweh** will not hold him guiltless that taketh his name in vain.

Deuteronomy 10:8
At that time **Yahweh** separated the tribe of Levi, to bear the ark of the covenant of **Yahweh**, to stand before **Yahweh** to minister unto him, and to bless **in his name**, unto this day.

Deuteronomy 18:5
For **Yahweh** thy God hath chosen him out of all thy tribes, to stand to **minister in the name of Yahweh**, him and his sons for ever.

Deuteronomy 18:7
Then he shall **minister in the name of Yahweh** his God, as all his brethren the Levites do, which stand there before **Yahweh**.

Deuteronomy 18:19
And it shall come to pass, that whosoever will not hearken unto my words which he shall speak **in my name**, I will require it of him.

Deuteronomy 18:20
But the prophet, which shall presume to speak a word **in my name**, which I have not commanded him to speak, or that shall speak in the name of other gods, even that prophet shall die.

Deuteronomy 21:5
And the priests the sons of Levi shall come near; for them **Yahweh** thy God hath chosen to minister unto him, and to **bless in the name of Yahweh**; and by their word shall every controversy and every stroke be tried:

Deuteronomy 28:10
And all people of the earth shall see that thou art **called by the**

name of Yahweh; and they shall be afraid of thee.

Deuteronomy 32:3
Because I will **publish the name of Yahweh**: ascribe ye greatness unto our God.

JOSHUA

Joshua 9:9
And they said unto him, From a very far country thy servants are come because of **the name of Yahweh** thy God: for we have heard the fame of him, and all that he did in Egypt,

JUDGES

Judges 13:18
And the angel of **Yahweh** said unto him, Why askest thou thus after **my name**, seeing it is secret?

SAMUEL

1 Samuel 17:45
Then said David to the Philistine, Thou comest to me with a sword, and with a spear, and with a shield: but I come to thee in **the name of Yahweh** of hosts, the God of the armies of Israel, whom thou hast defied.

1 Samuel 24:21
Swear now therefore unto me by **Yahweh**, that thou wilt not cut off my seed after me, and that thou wilt not destroy **my name** out of my father's house.

2 Samuel 6:2
And David arose, and went with all the people that were with him from Baale of Judah, to bring up from thence **the ark of God, whose name is called by the name of Yahweh** of hosts that dwelleth between the cherubims.

2 Samuel 6:18
And as soon as David had made an end of offering burnt offerings and peace offerings, he blessed the people **in the name**

of Yahweh of hosts.

2 Samuel 7:13
He shall build an house for **my name**, and I will stablish the throne of his kingdom for ever.

KINGS

1 Kings 5:5
And, behold, I purpose to build an house unto **the name of Yahweh** my God, as **Yahweh** spake unto David my father, saying, Thy son, whom I will set upon thy throne in thy room, he shall build an house unto **my name**.

1 Kings 8:16
Since the day that I brought forth my people Israel out of Egypt, I chose no city out of all the tribes of Israel to build an house, that **my name** might be therein; but I chose David to be over my people Israel.

1 Kings 8:18
And **Yahweh** said unto David my father, Whereas it was in thine heart to build an house unto **my name**, thou didst well that it was in thine heart.

1 Kings 8:19
Nevertheless thou shalt not build the house; but thy son that shall come forth out of thy loins, he shall build the house unto **my name**.

1 Kings 8:29
That thine eyes may be open toward this house night and day, even toward the place of which thou hast said, **My name** shall be there: that thou mayest hearken unto the prayer which thy servant shall make toward this place.

1 Kings 9:3
And **Yahweh** said unto him, I have heard thy prayer and thy supplication, that thou hast made before me: I have hallowed this house, which thou hast built, to put **my name** there for ever; and mine eyes and mine heart shall be there perpetually.

1 Kings 9:7
Then will I cut off Israel out of the land which I have given them; and this house, which I have hallowed for **my name**, will I cast out of my sight; and Israel shall be a proverb and a byword among all people:

1 Kings 10:1
And when the queen of Sheba heard of the fame of Solomon concerning **the name of Yahweh**, she came to prove him with hard questions.

1 Kings 18:24
And call ye on the name of your gods, and I will **call on the name of Yahweh**: and the God that answereth by fire, let him be God. And all the people answered and said, It is well spoken.

1 Kings 18:32
And with the stones he built an altar **in the name of Yahweh**: and he made a trench about the altar, as great as would contain two measures of seed.

CHRONICLES

1 Chronicles 16:2
And when David had made an end of offering the burnt offerings and the peace offerings, he blessed the people **in the name of Yahweh**.

1 Chronicles 16:10
Glory ye in **his holy name**: let the heart of them rejoice that seek **Yahweh**.

1 Chronicles 16:35
And say ye, Save us, O God of our salvation, and gather us together, and deliver us from the nations, that we may give thanks to **thy holy name**, and glory in thy praise.

1 Chronicles 22:19
Now set your heart and your soul to seek **Yahweh** your God; arise therefore, and build ye the sanctuary of **Yahweh** God, to bring the **ark of the covenant of Yahweh**, and the holy vessels of God, into the house that is to be built to **the name of Yahweh**.

1 Chronicles 23:13

…and Aaron was separated, that he should sanctify the most holy things, he and his sons for ever, to burn incense before **Yahweh**, to minister unto him, and to bless **in his name** for ever.

1 Chronicles 29:16

O **YAHWEH** our God, all this store that we have prepared to build thee an house for thine **holy name** cometh of thine hand, and is all thine own.

1 Chronicles 22:10

He shall build an house for **my name**; and he shall be my son, and I will be his father; and I will establish the throne of his kingdom over Israel for ever.

2 Chronicles 2:1

And Solomon determined to build an house for **the name of Yahweh**, and an house for his kingdom.

2 Chronicles 7:14

If my people, which are **called by my name**, shall humble themselves, and pray, and seek my face, and turn from their wicked ways; then will I hear from heaven, and will forgive their sin, and will heal their land.

2 Chronicles 7:16

For now have I chosen and sanctified this house, that **my name** may be there for ever: and mine eyes and mine heart shall be there perpetually.

2 Chronicles 18:15

And the king said to him, How many times shall I adjure thee that thou say nothing but the truth to me **in the name of Yahweh**?

NEHEMIAH

Nehemiah 1:9

But if ye turn unto me, and keep my commandments, and do them; though there were of you cast out unto the uttermost part of the heaven, yet will I gather them from thence, and will bring them unto the place that I have chosen to set **my name** there.

JOB

Job 1:21
And said, Naked came I out of my mother's womb, and naked shall I return thither: **Yahweh** gave, and **Yahweh** hath taken away; blessed be **the name of Yahweh**.

PSALMS

Psalm 7:17
I will praise **Yahweh** according to his righteousness: and will sing praise to **the name of Yahweh** most high.

Psalm 20:7
Some trust in chariots, and some in horses: but we will **remember the name of Yahweh** our God.

Psalm 33:21
For our heart shall rejoice in him, because we have trusted in **his holy name**.

Psalm 89:24
But my faithfulness and my mercy shall be with him: and **in my name** shall his horn be exalted.

Psalm 91:14
Because he hath set his love upon me, therefore will I deliver him: I will set him on high, because he hath known **my name**.

Psalm 102:15
So the nations shall fear **the name of Yahweh**, and all the kings of the earth thy glory.

Psalm 102:21
To **declare the name of Yahweh** in Zion, and his praise in Jerusalem;

Psalm 103:1
Bless **Yahweh**, O my soul: and all that is within me, bless **his holy name**.

Psalm 105:3
Glory ye in **his holy name**: let the heart of them rejoice that seek **Yahweh**.

Psalm 106:47

Save us, O **YAHWEH** our God, and gather us from among the nations, to give thanks unto **thy holy name**, and to triumph in thy praise.

Psalm 111:9

He sent redemption unto his people: he hath commanded his covenant for ever: **holy and reverend is his name.**

Psalm 113:1

Praise ye **Yahweh**. Praise, O ye servants of **Yahweh**, praise **the name of Yahweh**.

Psalm 113:2

Blessed be **the name of Yahweh** from this time forth and for evermore.

Psalm 116:4

Then called I **upon the name of Yahweh**; O **YAHWEH**, I beseech thee, deliver my soul.

Psalm 116:13

I will take the cup of **Salvation [*Yesu*]**, and **call upon the name of Yahweh**.

Psalm 116:17

I will offer to thee the sacrifice of thanksgiving, and will **call upon the name of Yahweh**.

Psalm 118:10-12

All nations compassed me about: but **in the name of Yahweh** will I destroy them.

They compassed me about; yea, they compassed me about: but **in the name of Yahweh** I will destroy them.

They compassed me about like bees: they are quenched as the fire of thorns: for **in the name of Yahweh** I will destroy them.

Psalm 118:26

Blessed be he that cometh **in the name of Yahweh**: we have blessed you out of the house of **Yahweh**.

Psalm 124:8

Our help is **in the name of Yahweh**, who made heaven and earth.

Psalm 135:1
Praise ye **Yahweh**. Praise ye **the name of Yahweh**; praise him, O ye servants of **Yahweh**.

Psalm 145:21
My mouth shall speak the praise of **Yahweh**: and let all flesh bless **his holy name** for ever and ever.

Psalm 148:5
Let them praise **the name of Yahweh**: for he commanded, and they were created.

Psalm 148:13
Let them praise **the name of Yahweh**: for his name alone is excellent; his glory is above the earth and heaven.

PROVERBS

Proverbs 18:10
The name of Yahweh is a strong tower: the righteous runneth into it, and is safe.

ISAIAH

Isaiah 29:23
But when he seeth his children, the work of mine hands, in the midst of him, they shall **sanctify my name**, and sanctify the Holy One of Jacob, and shall fear the God of Israel.

Isaiah 30:27
Behold, **the name of Yahweh** cometh from far, burning with his anger, and the burden thereof is heavy: his lips are full of indignation, and his tongue as a devouring fire:

Isaiah 41:25
I have raised up one from the north, and he shall come: from the rising of the sun shall he **call upon my name**: and he shall come upon princes as upon morter, and as the potter treadeth clay.

Isaiah 42:8
I am **Yahweh**: that is **my name**: and my glory will I not give to another, neither my praise to graven images.

Isaiah 43:6-8
I will say to the north, Give up; and to the south, Keep not back: bring my sons from far, and my daughters from the ends of the earth;

Even every one that is **called by my name**: for I have created him for my glory, I have formed him; yea, I have made him.

Bring forth the blind people that have eyes, and the deaf that have ears.

Isaiah 48:10-12
Behold, I have refined thee, but not with silver; I have chosen thee in the furnace of affliction.

For mine own sake, even for mine own sake, will I do it: for how should **my name** be polluted? and I will not give my glory unto another.

Hearken unto me, O Jacob and Israel, my called; I am he; I am the first, I also am the last.

Isaiah 49:1-3
Listen, O isles, unto me; and hearken, ye people, from far; **Yahweh** hath called me from the womb; from the bowels of my mother hath he made mention of **my name**.

And he hath made my mouth like a sharp sword; in the shadow of his hand hath he hid me, and made me a polished shaft; in his quiver hath he hid me;

And said unto me, Thou art my servant, O Israel, in whom I will be glorified.

Isaiah 50:10
Who is among you that feareth **Yahweh**, that obeyeth the voice of his servant, that walketh in darkness, and hath no light? let him trust **in the name of Yahweh**, and stay upon his God.

Isaiah 52:5-6
Now therefore, what have I here, saith **Yahweh**, that my people is taken away for nought? they that rule over them make them to howl, saith **Yahweh**; and **my name** continually every day is blasphemed.
Therefore my people **shall know my name**: therefore they shall know in that day that I am he that doth speak: behold, it is I.

Isaiah 56:6
Also the sons of the stranger, that join themselves to **Yahweh**, to serve him, and to love **the name of Yahweh**, to be his servants, every one that **keepeth the sabbath** from polluting it, and taketh hold of my covenant;

Isaiah 59:19
So shall they fear **the name of Yahweh** from the west, and his glory from the rising of the sun. When the enemy shall come in like a flood, the Spirit of **Yahweh** shall lift up a standard against him.

Isaiah 60:9
Surely the isles shall wait for me, and the ships of Tarshish first, to bring thy sons from far, their silver and their gold with them, unto **the name of Yahweh** thy God, and to the Holy One of Israel, because he hath glorified thee.

Isaiah 65:1
I am sought of them that asked not for me; I am found of them that sought me not: I said, Behold me, behold me, unto a nation that was not **called by my name**.

JEREMIAH

Jeremiah 3:17
At that time they shall call Jerusalem the throne of **Yahweh**; and all the nations shall be gathered unto it, to **the name of Yahweh**, to Jerusalem: neither shall they walk any more after the imagination of their evil heart.

Jeremiah 7:11
Is this house, which is **called by my name**, become a den of robbers in your eyes? Behold, even I have seen it, saith **Yahweh**.

Jeremiah 7:30
For the children of Judah have done evil in my sight, saith **Yahweh**: they have set their abominations in the house which is **called by my name**, to pollute it.

Jeremiah 12:16
And it shall come to pass, if they will diligently learn the ways of my people, to swear by **my name**, **Yahweh** liveth; as they taught my people to swear by Baal; then shall they be built in the midst

of my people.

Jeremiah 14:14
Then **Yahweh** said unto me, The prophets prophesy lies **in my name**: I sent them not, neither have I commanded them, neither spake unto them: they prophesy unto you a false vision and divination, and a thing of nought, and the deceit of their heart.

Jeremiah 14:15
Therefore thus saith **Yahweh** concerning the prophets that prophesy **in my name**, and I sent them not, yet they say, Sword and famine shall not be in this land; By sword and famine shall those prophets be consumed.

Jeremiah 16:21
Therefore, behold, I will this once cause them to know, I will cause them to know mine hand and my might; and **they shall know that my name is Yahweh.**

Jeremiah 23:25
I have heard what the prophets said, that prophesy lies **in my name**, saying, I have dreamed, I have dreamed.

Jeremiah 23:27
Which think to **cause my people to forget my name** by their dreams which they tell every man to his neighbour, as their fathers have **forgotten my name** for Baal.

Jeremiah 26:16
Then said the princes and all the people unto the priests and to the prophets; This man is not worthy to die: for he hath spoken to us **in the name of Yahweh** our God.

Jeremiah 27:15
For I have not sent them, saith **Yahweh**, yet they prophesy a lie **in my name**; that I might drive you out, and that ye might perish, ye, and the prophets that prophesy unto you.

Jeremiah 29:9
For they prophesy falsely unto you **in my name**: I have not sent them, saith **Yahweh**.

Jeremiah 32:34
But they set their abominations in the house, which is **called by my name**, to defile it.

Jeremiah 44:26
Therefore hear ye the word of **Yahweh**, all Judah that dwell in the land of Egypt; Behold, I have sworn by my great name, saith **Yahweh**, that **my name** shall no more be named in the mouth of any man of Judah in all the land of Egypt, saying, Lord **Yahweh** liveth.

EZEKIEL

Ezekiel 20:39
As for you, O house of Israel, thus saith Lord **Yahweh**; Go ye, serve ye every one his idols, and hereafter also, if ye will not hearken unto me: but pollute ye **my holy name** no more with your gifts, and with your idols.

Ezekiel 36:20
And when they entered unto the nations, whither they went, they profaned **my holy name**, when they said to them, These are the people of **Yahweh**, and are gone forth out of his land.

Ezekiel 36:21
But I had pity for **mine holy name**, which the house of Israel had profaned among the nations, whither they went.

Ezekiel 39:7
So will I make **my holy name** known in the midst of my people Israel; and I will not let them pollute **my holy name** any more: and the nations shall know that I am **Yahweh**, the Holy One in Israel.

Ezekiel 39:25
Therefore thus saith Lord **Yahweh**; Now will I bring again the captivity of Jacob, and have mercy upon the whole house of Israel, and will be jealous for **my holy name**;

Ezekiel 43:7
And he said unto me, Son of man, the place of my throne, and the place of the soles of my feet, where I will dwell in the midst of the children of Israel for ever, and **my holy name**, shall the house of Israel no more defile …

JOEL

Joel 2:26
And ye shall eat in plenty, and be satisfied, and praise **the name of Yahweh** your God, that hath dealt wondrously with you: and my people shall never be ashamed.

Joel 2:32
And it shall come to pass, that whosoever shall **call on the name of Yahweh** shall be delivered: for in mount Zion and in Jerusalem shall be deliverance, as **Yahweh** hath said, and in the remnant whom **Yahweh** shall call.

AMOS

Amos 9:12
That they may possess the remnant of Edom, and of all the nations, which are **called by my name**, saith **Yahweh** that doeth this.

MICAH

Micah 4:5
For all people will walk every one in the name of his god, and we will walk **in the name of Yahweh** our God for ever and ever.

Micah 5:4
And he shall stand and feed in the strength of **Yahweh**, in the majesty of **the name of Yahweh** his God; and they shall abide: for now shall he be great unto the ends of the earth.

ZEPHANIAH

Zephaniah 3:9
For then will I turn to the people a pure language, that they may all **call upon the name of Yahweh**, to serve him with one consent.

Zephaniah 3:12
I will also leave in the midst of thee an afflicted and poor people, and they shall trust **in the name of Yahweh**.

Zechariah 10:12
And I will strengthen them in **Yahweh**; and they shall walk up

and down **in his name**, saith **Yahweh**.

Zechariah 13:9
And I will bring the third part through the fire, and will refine them as silver is refined, and will try them as gold is tried: they shall call on **my name**, and I will hear them: I will say, It is my people: and they shall say, **Yahweh** is my God.

MALACHI

Malachi 1:6
A son honoureth his father, and a servant his master: if then I be a father, where is mine honour? and if I be a master, where is my fear? saith **Yahweh** of hosts unto you, O priests, that despise **my name**. And ye say, Wherein have we despised thy name?

Malachi 1:11
For from the rising of the sun even unto the going down of the same **my name** shall be great among the Gentiles; and in every place incense shall be offered unto **my name**, and a pure offering: for **my name** shall be great among the nations, saith **Yahweh** of hosts.

Malachi 1:14
But cursed be the deceiver, which hath in his flock a male, and voweth, and sacrificeth unto **Yahweh** a corrupt thing: for I am a great King, saith **Yahweh** of hosts, and **my name** is dreadful among the nations.

Malachi 2:2
If ye will not hear, and if ye will not lay it to heart, to give glory unto **my name**, saith **Yahweh** of hosts, I will even send a curse upon you, and I will curse your blessings: yea, I have cursed them already, because ye do not lay it to heart.

Malachi 2:5
My covenant was with him of life and peace; and I gave them to him for the fear wherewith he feared me, and was afraid before **my name**.

Malachi 4:2
But unto you that fear **my name** shall the Sun of righteousness arise with healing in his wings; and ye shall go forth, and grow up as calves of the stall.

MATTHEW

Matthew 12:21
And **in his name** shall the Gentiles trust.

Matthew 18:5
And whoso shall receive one such little child **in my name** receiveth me.

Matthew 18:20
For where two or three are gathered together **in my name**, there am I in the midst of them.

Matthew 21:9
And the multitudes that went before, and that followed, cried, saying, Hosanna to the son of David: Blessed is he that cometh **in the name of Yahweh**; Hosanna in the highest.

Matthew 23:39
For I say unto you, Ye shall not see me henceforth, till ye shall say, Blessed is he that cometh **in the name of Yahweh**.

MARK

Mark 9:37
Whosoever shall receive one of such children **in my name**, receiveth me: and whosoever shall receive me, receiveth not me, but him that sent me.

Mark 9:39
But **Yesu** said, Forbid him not: for there is no man which shall do a miracle **in my name**, that can lightly speak evil of me.

Mark 9:41
For whosoever shall give you a cup of water to drink **in my name**, because ye belong to Christ, verily I say unto you, he shall not lose his reward.

Mark 11:9
And they that went before, and they that followed, cried, saying, Hosanna; Blessed is he that cometh **in the name of Yahweh**:

Mark 11:10
Blessed be the kingdom of our father David, that cometh **in the name of Yahweh**: Hosanna in the highest.

Mark 16:17
And these signs shall follow them that believe; **In my name** shall
they cast out devils; they shall speak with new tongues;

LUKE

Luke 9:48
And said unto them, Whosoever shall receive this child **in my
name** receiveth me: and whosoever shall receive me receiveth
him that sent me: for he that is least among you all, the same shall
be great.

Luke 13:35
Behold, your house is left unto you desolate: and verily I say unto
you, Ye shall not see me, until the time come when ye shall say,
Blessed is he that cometh **in the name of Yahweh**.

Luke 19:38
Saying, Blessed be the King that cometh **in the name of
Yahweh**: peace in heaven, and glory in the highest.

Luke 24:47
And that repentance and remission of sins should be preached **in
his name** among all nations, beginning at Jerusalem.

JOHN

John 2:23
Now when he was in Jerusalem at the passover, in the feast day,
many **believed in his name**, when they saw the miracles which
he did.

John 3:18
He that believeth on him is not condemned: but he that believeth
not is **condemned** already, **because he hath not believed in
the name of the only begotten Son of God**.

John 12:13
Took branches of palm trees, and went forth to meet him, and
cried, Hosanna: Blessed is the King of Israel that cometh **in the
name of Yahweh**.

John 14:13
And whatsoever ye shall ask **in my name**, that will I do, that the

Father may be glorified in the Son.

John 14:14
If ye shall ask any thing **in my name**, I will do it.

John 14:26
But the Comforter, which is the Holy Ghost, whom the Father
will send **in my name**, he shall teach you all things, and bring all
things to your remembrance, whatsoever I have said unto you.

John 15:16
Ye have not chosen me, but I have chosen you, and ordained you,
that ye should go and bring forth fruit, and that your fruit should
remain: that whatsoever ye shall ask of the Father **in my name**,
he may give it you.

John 16:23
And in that day ye shall ask me nothing. Verily, verily, I say unto
you, Whatsoever ye shall ask the Father **in my name**, he will
give it you.

John 16:24
Hitherto have ye asked nothing **in my name**: ask, and ye shall
receive, that your joy may be full.

John 16:26
At that day ye shall ask **in my name**: and I say not unto you,
that I will pray the Father for you:

ACTS

Acts 2:21
And it shall come to pass, that whosoever shall **call on the
name of Yahweh** shall be saved.

Acts 2:38
Then Peter said unto them, Repent, and be baptized every one of
you **in the name of Yesu** Christ **for the remission of sins**,
and ye shall receive the gift of the Holy Ghost.

Acts 3:6
Then Peter said, Silver and gold have I none; but such as I have
give I thee: **In the name of Yesu** Christ of Nazareth rise up
and walk.

Acts 3:16
And his name through **faith in his name** hath made this man strong, whom ye see and know: yea, the faith which is by him hath given him this perfect soundness in the presence of you all.

Acts 4:10-12
Be it known unto you all, and to all the people of Israel, that **by the name of Yesu Christ** of Nazareth, whom ye crucified, whom God raised from the dead, even by him doth this man stand here before you whole.

This is the stone which was set at nought of you builders, which is become the head of the corner. **Neither is there salvation in any other**: for there is **none other name** under heaven given among men, **whereby we must be saved**.

Acts 4:18
And they called them, and commanded them not to speak at all nor teach **in the name of Yesu**.

Acts 5:40
And to him they agreed: and when they had called the apostles, and beaten them, they commanded that they should not speak **in the name of Yesu** ...

Acts 8:12
But when they believed Philip preaching the things concerning the kingdom of God, and **the name of Yesu** Christ, they were baptized, both men and women.

Acts 8:16
For as yet he [*the Holy Ghost*] was fallen upon none of them: only they were baptized **in the name of Yahweh Yesu**.

Acts 9:15
But **Yahweh** said unto him, Go thy way: for he is a chosen vessel unto me, to bear **my name** before the Gentiles, and kings, and the children of Israel:

Acts 9:27
But Barnabas took him, and brought him to the apostles, and declared unto them how he had seen the **Yahweh** in the way, and that he had spoken to him, and how he had preached boldly at Damascus **in the name of Yesu**.

Acts 9:29
And he spake boldly **in the name of Yahweh Yesu** …

Acts 10:48
And he commanded them to be baptized **in the name of Yahweh**. Then prayed they him to tarry certain days.

Acts 15:17
That the residue of men might seek after **Yahweh**, and all the Gentiles, upon whom **my name** is called, saith **Yahweh**, who doeth all these things.

Acts 16:18
And this did she many days. But Paul, being grieved, turned and said to the spirit, I command thee **in the name of Yesu** Christ to come out of her. And he came out the same hour.

Acts 19:5
When they heard this, they were baptized **in the name of Yahweh Yesu**.

Acts 19:13
Then certain of the vagabond Jews, exorcists, took upon them to call over them which had evil spirits **the name of Yahweh Yesu**, saying, We adjure you by **Yesu** whom Paul preacheth.

Acts 19:17
And this was known to all the Jews and Greeks also dwelling at Ephesus; and fear fell on them all, and **the name of Yahweh Yesu** was magnified.

Acts 22:16
And now why tarriest thou? arise, and be baptized, and wash away thy sins, **calling on the name of Yahweh**.

ROMANS

Romans 9:17
For the scripture saith unto Pharaoh, Even for this same purpose have I raised thee up, that I might shew my power in thee, and that **my name** might be declared throughout all the earth.

Romans 10:13
For whosoever shall **call upon the name of Yahweh** shall be saved.

CORINTHIANS

1 Corinthians 1:2
Unto the church of God which is at Corinth, to them that are **sanctified in Christ Yesu**, called to be saints, with all that in every place **call upon the name of Yesu** Christ our **Yahweh**, both their's and our's:

1 Corinthians 6:11
And such were some of you: but ye are washed, but ye are sanctified, but ye are justified **in the name of Yahweh Yesu**, and by the Spirit of our God.

PHILIPPIANS

Philippians 2:9-12

Wherefore God also hath highly exalted him, and given him a **name** which is **above every name**:
That at **the name of Yesu** every knee should bow, of things in heaven, and things in earth, and things under the earth;

And that every tongue should confess that **Yesu Christ is Yahweh**, to the glory of God the Father.

Wherefore, my beloved, as ye have always obeyed, not as in my presence only, but now much more in my absence, work out your own salvation with fear and trembling.

COLOSSIANS

Colossians 3:17
And whatsoever ye do in word or deed, do all **in the name of Yahweh Yesu**, giving thanks to God and the Father by him.

JAMES

James 5:10
Take, my brethren, the prophets, who have spoken **in the name of Yahweh**, for an example of suffering affliction, and of patience.

James 5:14-15
Is any sick among you? let him call for the elders of the church;

and let them pray over him, anointing him with oil **in the name of Yahweh**:

And the prayer of faith shall save the sick, and **Yahweh** shall raise him up; and if he have committed sins, they shall be forgiven him.

REVELATION

Revelation 2:13

I know thy works, and where thou dwellest, even where Satan's seat is: and thou holdest fast **my name**, and hast not denied my faith, even in those days wherein Antipas was my faithful witness, who was slain among you, where Satan dwelleth.

Revelation 3:7-8

And to the angel of the church in Philadelphia write; These things saith he that is holy, he that is true, **he that hath the key of David, he that openeth, and no man shutteth; and shutteth, and no man openeth**;
I know thy works: behold, I have **set before thee an open door**, and no man can shut it: for thou hast a little strength, and hast kept my word, and hast **not denied my name**.

John 3:18
He that believeth on him is not condemned:

but **he that believeth not is condemned** already, **because he hath not believed in** *the name* of the only begotten Son of God.

NAKED TRUTH

YESU'S WAY AND ATTITUDE

SERMON ON THE MOUNT

Matthew 5

[1] And seeing the multitudes, he went up into a mountain: and when he was set, his disciples came unto him:
[2] And he opened his mouth, and taught them, saying,

[3] Blessed [*happy, fortunate*] are the *beggars* in spirit: for theirs is the kingdom of heaven.

[4] Blessed are they that mourn: for they shall be comforted.

[5] Blessed are the meek: for they shall inherit the earth.

[6] Blessed are they which do hunger and thirst after righteousness: for they shall be filled.

[7] Blessed are the merciful: for they shall obtain mercy.

[8] Blessed are the pure in heart: for they shall see God.

[9] Blessed are the peacemakers: for they shall be called the children of God.

[10] Blessed are they which are persecuted for righteousness' sake: for theirs is the kingdom of heaven.

[11] Blessed are ye, when men shall revile you, and persecute you, and shall say all manner of evil against you falsely, for my sake. [cf. John 15:21, Greek, "***Because of my name***."].

[12] Rejoice, and be exceeding glad: for great is your reward in heaven: for so persecuted they the prophets which were before you.

[13] Ye are the salt of the earth: but if the salt have lost his savour, wherewith shall it be salted? it is thenceforth good for nothing, but to be cast out, and to be trodden under foot of men.

[14] Ye are the light of the world. A city that is set on an hill cannot be hid.
[15] Neither do men light a candle, and put it under a bushel, but on a candlestick; and it giveth light unto all that are in the house.
[16] Let your light so shine before men, that they may see your good works, and glorify your Father which is in heaven.

[17] Think not that I am come to destroy the law, or the prophets: I am not come to destroy, but to fulfil.
[18] For verily I say unto you, Till heaven and earth pass, one ***Yod*** or one tittle **shall in no wise pass from the law** [*Torah/Bible*], till all be fulfilled. [cf. 1Chronicles 29:16, "O **Yahweh** our God...**thine holy name** is from thy *hand* (*yad*, ***Yod*** = Y)."]

[19] Whosoever therefore shall *loosen down* one of these least commandments, and shall teach men so, he shall be called the least in the kingdom of heaven: but whosoever shall do and teach them, the same shall be called great in the kingdom of heaven. [20] For I say unto you, That except your righteousness shall exceed the righteousness of the scribes and Pharisees, ye shall in no case enter into the kingdom of heaven.

UNCLOAKED

John 15

[20] Remember the word that I said unto you, The servant is not greater than his *master*. If they have persecuted me, they will also persecute you; if they have kept my saying, they will keep yours also.
[21] But all these things will they do unto you **because of my name**, because they know not him that sent me.

[22] If I had not come and spoken unto them, they had not had sin: but

"now they have no cloak for their sin."